AFRICAN PERFORMANCE REVIEW

Vol 1, nos 2&3, 2007

Editorial board

Editor
Dr Osita Okagbue,
Goldsmiths College,
University of London

Associate Editors
Dr Jumai Ewu,
University of Northampton
Dr Victor Ukaegbu,
University of Northampton

Reviews Editor
Dr Sam Kasule,
University of Derby

Advisory Board
Professor Dapo Adelugba,
University of Ibadan
Professor Eckhard Breitinger,
Bayreuth University
Professor Ossie Enekwe,
University of Nigeria, Nsukka
Professor Robert Gordon, Goldsmiths,
University of London
Professor Temple Hauptfleisch,
University of Stellenbosch
Professor Chimalum Nwankwo,
North Carolina A & T State University, Greensboro

Adonis & Abbey Publishers Ltd
P. O. Box43418
London, UK
SE11 4XZ

Copyright 2007© ISSN : 1753-5964
Adonis & Abbey Publishers Ltd

Cover design Ifeanyi F. Adibe

www.adonis-abbey.com

African Performance Review: Notes for contributors

African Performance Review is a bi-annual journal of the African Theatre Association (AfTA) dedicated to publishing, disseminating and encouraging high quality research and information on theatres and performance in Africa and the African Diaspora. The journal publishes articles, review articles and reviews on all aspects of African performance and theatre.

Articles are accepted and published on the recommendation of referees. Manuscripts should be original and unpublished contributions, and should not be under submission to another publication. Articles should not normally exceed 5000 words, and must be typed double-spaced with wide margins. In order to be considered, two copies of the manuscript and a disk (Word 6 compatible) or e-mail attachment should be submitted.

Contributors should use the Harvard Style. All references are included in the text and are indicated by surname(s) or author(s), year of publication and page number(s) in brackets,: eg. (Kerr, 1995:33)

Each article should be accompanied by an abstract of 100-150 words on a separate sheet.

Manuscripts should be sent to the Editor, African Performance Review, Department of Drama, Goldsmiths, University of London, SE14 6NW United Kingdom. Tel: +44 (0)207 919-7581. Enquiries and communication should be sent by e-mail to AfTA@gold.ac.uk

For subscription inquiries, contact: sales@adonis-abbey.com

African Journal of Business and Economic Research

AJBER

Annual Subscription Rates

Companies/orgs./institutions: £200
(including access to the online editions)

Individuals: hardcopy only: £50
Individuals: online and Print: £60
Individuals: Online only: £30

Retail sales:
Individuals (print) £20 (+ P&P)
Online £10 per issue

For subscription and advertisement enquiries contact:

sales@adonis-abbey.com
Phone: +44 (0) 20 7793 8893

Adonis & Abbey Publishers Ltd
P.O. Box 43418,
London
SE11 4XZ
United Kingdom

To contribute to
African Perfomance Review
please contact:
AfTA@gold.ac.uk

Signifying Systems in Traditional African Theatre Aesthetics: The *Girinya* Ritual Dance of the Tiv people of Nigeria

Gowon Ama Doki, PhD.

Department of Theatre Arts, Benue State University, Makurdi

Abstract

Several theatre traditions exist in Africa that are not even recognized and registered as theatres in the strict professional sense of the word. The electronic age has appropriated every thing, including research, to computerized evaluation, leaving issues of traditional complexion to wallow in the pity and mercy of their respective custodians. The implication therefore is that, serious and rich theatre traditions may soon go extinct if nothing is done in the form of research to try and patronize and thus preserve these traditions. This paper is of the view that there exist exciting theatre traditions in Africa that use a wide range of sign systems to communicate and also pass across the aspiration and cultural ethos of Africans to the world. The hope therefore is that scholars should devote some time and effort to the study of some of these performances, one of which is the *Girinya* ritual dance theatre of the Tiv people of Nigeria.

Introduction

Traditional theatre encapsulates the existence, progress, development and maximum utilization of social and cultural institutions of a group as it concerns artistic recreation and re-evaluation of moral and social ethos. This covers a wide range of activities relating to the life styles of the people – their mode of worship, marriage relationship, farming, hunting, social mobilization, healthcare, economic potentialities, as well as cosmic and mystic beliefs. These are expressed through community outlets such as dance, music, song, mine, pantomime, costume, proxemic systems and many more codes (non-verbal) of communication. The totality of all of these, add up to the unique and edificatory experience known as theatre and drama. In a preface to a book on traditional theatre semiosis, Gbilekaa (2006: ix) observed that:

African traditional theatre refers to indigenous performances of Africa, festivals, masque dramaturgy, storytelling performances, puppetry, dances and comedies that abound in traditional society's area in a globalised world. These are performances or cultural activities of the people that have resisted the onslaught of western civilization. It takes into cognizance, the progress and development of an entire society, its aspirations and fears, its belief systems and moral and social ethics.

Traditional African society (the focus of this study) offers a rich menu of potent theatre traditions which through the ages has flourished into a unique specimen of scholarly resource. The *Girinya* ritual dance theatre is one of such fascinating theatres practised by the Tiv people of the present Benue State in Nigeria. It must also be placed on record that other neighbours of the Tiv also practise their own version of this same dance with their own peculiar dialectics. The Tiv people who are the ethnic group under examination here, have varying accounts of origin ascribed to them by different scholars. However, this is not peculiar to them as a people, but as Bur (1993:1) observed:

> The problem of studying the origin, character and development of ethnicity in Nigeria has been, and shall continue to be the vexatious task of historians, anthropologists, ethnographers, ethnomusicologists, theorists, administrators, academics and leaders.

He further adds that some of such accounts lack archaeological evidence and are shrouded in the plethora of oral versions, each making its claim of authenticity such that only students of history can settle the dispute through research. However, to Agber (1994:38):

> What appears certain is that, the speakers of the language once lived within an ancestral homeland referred to as Swem in the group's traditions of origin.

Swem above is said to be very important in the historical evolution of the Tiv because it became "something like the core of a confederacy exercising a loose control over a vast area of people speaking variants of the same language" (Ballard, 1971:53). Thus, to Agber, coherent Tiv history and the emergence of Tiv identity began to emerge at Swem. Population explosion, as well as the desire for more and suitable lands for production of sufficient food to feed the population, may have been the primary reasons for migration from Swem. Through their pilgrimage to the present land occupied by the Tiv people, a lot of groups and subgroups were met, many wars were fought, and, by implication, certain habits were borrowed, including several aspects of artistic creativity, of which dance is one. The import of this analysis within the context of this work is rightly to put into perspective, the environment of the traditional setting, its cultural antecedents and possible evolutionary trends in the development of its cultural resources and activities. Proceeding from this, we shall briefly examine the concept of the sign and its signifying systems.

The Sign

Signs constitute a major element in the structure of human relationships. The import of the sign is derived from what Jakobson calls *signans* and *signatum*. The *signans* is that which is immediately perceptible and the *signatum* that which is inferable, apprehensible (Shittu, 2004:60). According to Thomas (1978:237) "a sign is something that suggests the presence or existence of a fact, condition, or quality immediately evident". This "something" may be anything used to convey meaning to the mind. It could be a picture, a gesture, word, an object or mark. This rightly suggests that every message or conversation is made possible by use largely of signs. This, however, also expresses in a nutshell the functionality of signs and the use to which signs in themselves could be put by society and by individuals who may wish to evolve some communicative parameters based on the basic principles of the sign system. Hawkes (1977:127-28) has summarized these principles thus:

> These are the icon, something which functions as a sign by means of features of itself which resemble its objects; the index, something which functions as a sign by virtue of some sort of factual or causal connection with its object and the symbol, something which functions as a sign because of the rule of conventional or habitual association between itself and its object.

With this summary, Hawkes has identified three basic typologies of the sign - icon, index and symbol. However, these classifications are not absolute, pure and distinct as they appear; these signs usually interplay during performances producing diverse mixtures. Jakobson had in affirmation observed that we can have *symbolic icons* as well as *iconic symbols*. We can also have *indexical icons* or *iconic indexes* etcetera. The nature and context of usage often times enhance the quality, status and essence of the sign. The signifying systems in this performance are expressed through the process of dance, music, movement, costume, gestures and facial expressions. Let us therefore take a brief overview of the dance.

The *Girinya* Dance

Girinya is a war dance found among the Tiv, South of the Benue-Ishangev-Ya and Gaav. These clans have common boundaries with the small ethnic groups on the north of Cross River State, and this information is important because it is believed that this dance form was borrowed from these small groups that the Tiv collectively refer to as "Udam" (Pever-Ge 1985:106).

To premise this discussion on Pever-Ge's position as captured above gives the work some form of grounding in the sense that it establishes the nature of the *Girinya* dance as a war dance, its origin as a borrowed dance from Udam and an insight into the section of the Tiv people that perform the dance. "Udam" as a name is a Tiv coinage which refers to the upper Cross River (Obudu, Ogoja, Ugeb, Gakem). It is rather for convenience that the name is used in this work to refer to the above-mentioned communities. Nevertheless, it is noteworthy to add that the Kunav people in Vandeikya Local Government who share the closest of boundaries with the Cross River people are also very prominent in this ritual dance. The dance is symbolically a war dance, as virtually all elements or attributes of war are reflected in the different aspects that constitute the performance. Drawing inspiration from Bohannan's study of Tiv economy (1968:14), one could infer the origin and perhaps the reason for this dance. He contends that:

> The whole of Tivland is expanding with every demand for more land. Towards the edges of the country, each small lineage not only expands but also has a specific direction of migration. Until this system collided with enforceable British ideas of fixed boundaries, the lineages on the outside were preceding four or five miles a generation against the Udam people in the south and more rapidly than that in the north east where little opposition confronted them (in Pever-Ge (1985:106) .

Naturally, territorial expansion is synonymous with encroachment. As such, an atmosphere of hostility developed around this southward region, as the Tiv continued to acquire more land as against their "Udam" counterparts. It is noteworthy to mention at this point that the "Udam" clearly had this dance form which they refer to as '*Ogirinya*!' As a form of ritual dance, one had to provide a human head to become a member of the guild or to perform the burial ceremony of dead members. In line with this atmosphere of hostility already developed between the Udam of Cross River and the Tiv of Benue:

> The Udam usually cross over to the side of the Tiv people, to kill them and cut off their heads, either for the burial of a member of the Ogirinya guild or in order to become a member of the guild (Pever-Ge, 1985: 107).

The Tiv who could not sit and watch this continue, spied on the Udam and subsequently learnt the ritual and mode of performance of the enemy guild and today they perform an indigenous type of "*Ogirinya*" known as *Girinya*'. Thus it will not be an overstatement to contend that the *Girinya* dance emerged as a form of revenge against an enemy guild. The dire need to stem the killing of the Tiv brothers by the Udam people necessitated the emergence of this dance guild. This perhaps agrees with Ngugi wa Thiong'o's position that "a people's culture is the carrier of their economic and political life". (1983:8)

Performance Aesthetics

In trying to conceptualise African dances, Traore observed that:

> It is difficult to classify African dances. Each is linked with a specific human activity. Some dances may be reserved for those who have accomplished acts of valour (1972:57).

The *Girinya* dance thus falls under the category that is 'reserved for those who have accomplished acts of valour'. The dance is performed at two different levels: social and ritual levels. At the social level, *Girinya* is performed to honour august visitors to the land. It could also be performed at National Day Celebration and Christmas. As a ritual dance, *Girinya* is performed to honour departed or fallen warriors. Social performances are not usually formal. The music is usually provided; individual warriors come out in specific costumes and dance to the familiar rhythm. Those who are not members but know the dance steps are free to join the dance in a social performance. This stage is known as *"Numun Girinya"*. During the social performance,

> The horn blower gives a scintillating sound summoning the heroes (dancers) to the arena of performance. The heroes (dancers), machete in hand, answer the call with animalistic blabber that is not understood by non-initiates. This is quickly followed by the music. In response, the heroes move onto the stage from different points to do a dance movement (Mude, 1987: 46).

This, perhaps, is the much that can be performed during a social performance. The ritual performance is richer and more vivid and theatrically all-encompassing. Its performance is usually at the burial ceremony of a member (warrior-hero). A warrior-hero in Tivland is one who has gone out in defence of his fatherland, or one who has been able to acquire traditional condiments for the funeral ceremony of a fallen hero. When a member of the guild dies, his death is not announced until arrangements for his burial rites have been completed. Once completed, a *Nomkor* (big horn) sounds a notification blast, summoning the titled men together. The sound of the horn actually marks the official announcement of the warrior's death and it is only then that mourners are allowed to cry or shed tears. It also marks the beginning of a chain of activities that may last some days. On the day of performance proper, a shrine is erected somewhere around the compound covered with palm leaves and *anger* (traditional Tiv hand-woven cloth of black and white colours) around which a protocol of events seeking to cleanse both the dead member and living warriors from presumed stains is carried out. This shrine usually also houses the corpse of the dead warrior member. But for some health reasons, arising from modernization, only the accessories (cap, machete, beads, etc) of the dead member are kept under the shrine to represent the corpse (see Fig 1).

Fig. 1: An erected shrine housing the dead warrior's accessories

When this is constructed, all the *Anom-aior* (Tested Warriors) who had already undergone a cleansing ceremony to free them of the stains collected while prowling for funeral gadgets, now file out and walk stylishly round the shrine. For its structured performance, the *Girinya* dance, like any other traditional performance, is usually performed in an arena setting. Apart from the acrobatic nature of the dance which requires a wide space for its performance, the dance also calls for an intense interaction with the audience, something which can most effectively be achieved through the arena arrangement. In form, the *Girinya* dance ritual is in five connected sequences, what in literary terms can be known as 'scenes'. As mentioned earlier, Scene One, *Numum Girinya*, which serves as the opening glee or curtain raiser, involves the drummers who take up a position in the arena, with the dancers squatting at different positions round the arena behind the audience. The various horns dole out scintillating warlike sounds, accompanied by the drum and then the gong, with the clinging sound of the old tin filtering in to conclude the sound parade. The dancers (warriors) rush in from different directions and form a circle in front of the lone drummer. It should be noted here that this lone drummer communicates with the dancers through rhythm - hence the talking drum (Fig. 2).

Fig. 2. A lone drummer with head gear

With gentle and light movement, they dance anti-clockwise round the arena first, but as the music gradually rises to a crescendo, the dancers also step up the vigour with which they dance. They move faster, but nevertheless maintain uniformity in steps, tapping the ground with their bare feet to produce a pleasant sound from the *bibi* tied round their ankles, which blends well with the music. Thus far, any member of the audience can join, since it is purported to warm the arena and mobilize the people for the real performance. Songs are rarely used in this performance; the only human voice heard is the incomprehensible animalistic sounds by the warrior-dancers as they jerk up and down with a fixed gaze of vigour, a replica of a wounded wild beast. After the opening glee, the remaining part of the performance is restricted to only member-warrior-heroes. The only contribution left to other lay people is the cheer and applause.

The second scene or stage is graced by distinguished warrior-heroes armed with sharp glittering machetes. The machete is held in the right-hand, while the left holds the sheaths. Naturally, a dangling sharp machete gives a feeling of horror and danger. One who dances with a machete must therefore be dreaded. They (warrior-heroes) appear pointing the machetes to the east and then to the west to the rising and fading of the sun (Fig. 3). This performance is done with wild facial expressions of elaborated head nods, wide opened eyes, and violent jerking about the arena. Women who have also distinguished themselves in acts of valour can take part in this dance and be accorded burial ceremony similar to that accorded to men.

The third round or scene is essentially a solo performance, where a warrior – hero comes out to narrate the story of his valour, using the music and rhythm of the drum. Every warrior has a pet name that is coded between the warrior and the lead trumpeter (*Nomkor*). The trumpeter calls the warrior with such a coded name; he jumps in from amongst the audience with mild emotions and excitement. He prowls around the arena looking towards the east and west, with an eventual sharp step towards the drummer. He brandishes the machete as if threatening to cut off the drummer's head and finally settles for his dance. Movement at this time consists of elaborate and vigorous thrusting of the body and leg movement to the dictates of the drum. With an abrupt seizure of sound from the music stand, the dancer lies flat on the ground, and another member-hero appears almost immediately, places the flat blade across the neck of the prostrate figure, mimetic of the act of beheading a man. This episode continues until all the heroes appear on the stage.

Fig. 3 A warrior hero points the machete to the sun

The fourth stage is the *Gber girinya* stage where a goat is tied to a stake and a mandated member warrior cuts off the head of the goat with one stroke. No other person apart from the authorized can attempt to carry out this exercise. The chosen member, because he has the mandate of the other members, can perform this task with ease. The audience and other members of the guild stand in admiration of this personal display of skill by the chosen one while they also pray for a neat cut, for failure means not only a loss to the individual but the entire clan from which he is chosen. The drum beat directs his movement and he moves elegantly around the arena taking occasional long strides towards the goat with bulging bloodshot eyes. This movement is repeated until he is fully satisfied, and ready for action. The music ceases, he looks up and down, throws the machete up and as he catches it mid-air, he then cuts neatly through the goat, amidst cheers from the audience and fellow members (Fig. 4).

Fig 4: A mandated warrior severing the head of the goat from the body.

It is pertinent to add at this point that if you are wrongly chosen, you can not as much as inflict a cut on the goat skin, no matter your strength and valour. In most cases, the mandated person cuts cleanly without any problem. On the other hand, if the person chosen fails to cut cleanly, his machete is seized and he is temporarily suspended from the membership of the warriors' circle until he pays a fine as may be decided by the priest. After payment he undergoes some purification rites before his final reinstatement.

The final stage of a *Girinya* performance is the eating of a meal. The warriors are fed by the priest. The food consists of slices of yam put in a pot with palm oil and some pepper. The mesh is put on a heath and allowed to stay for a few seconds. The priest picks up the slices with the tip of a knife, holds it out for all to see while the warrior to be fed stands out, hands behind his back. He takes the piece of yam with his teeth. This process of feeding the warriors continues until every warrior physically present is fed. Once this is done, the deceased hero would be laid to rest.

Fig. 5: The chief priest feeding a warrior

In the past, *Girinya* costume usually consisted of a skirt made of raffia leaves and a hat made by putting together pieces of locally woven cloths sewn in accordance with the size of the wearer's head. The hat is stocked with pines of the porcupine to give it a fierce appearance and enable the warrior present the figure of a man to be dreaded. The costume also usually comprises *bibi* (shakers) tied round the ankles. Today, however, because *Girinya* is not only a sacred performance, the costuming has been modified to accommodate some liberal form of dress. The warriors wear pairs of shorts or trousers with wrappers tied into a knot on the backside. Semi-singlet is used for the chest while the lead dancer may wear a gown entirely covered by *bibi* seeds. This dress is also extended to cover the head of the warrior with holes bored to enhance his sight. The entire costume gives him an appearance of a wounded lion. All these constitute theatrical aesthetics with which to appreciate the *girinya* dance and thus explore in semiotic terms the measure of its cultural and social relevance as it relates to the Tiv cultural world view.

Signifying Systems in *Girinya* Dance

In semiotic terms, dance features prominently as a cultural signifier with a lot of social and religious messages which interpret the world view and cosmological values of the Tiv and other African peoples. Dance is a technical and essential aspect of theatre. Through dance, performers adapt intelligently their bodies to the rhythm of the musical instrument. Dance is the movement of the body to a sound in a rhythmic pattern. Through this serious concentration, meanings are conveyed to the audience. This is understood when the audience pays much attention to the dance expression, atmosphere or mood and movement on stage. Ogbonna (1991:45) posits that:

> Dance as an aspect of human communication is more logical, technical and efficient when members of the chorus reduce their chants, songs and other verbal expressions or almost all their dialogue to mime. In mime verbal expression or all of the dialogue presented are reduced to conventions (or symbols) and body movements with the utilization of signs.

Worth mentioning is also the fact that music and dance are not just recreational activities in Tivland but as fundamental phenomena, they permeate all aspects of Tiv life. Hagher (1993:6) rightly observes that:

> Music and dance do not only serve the purpose of social interaction as well as a school for intellectual stimulation, they also control normative behavior. Sometimes they serve as a medium for social protest and even sanction deviant behavior.

Most of the movements in this dance are significantly relevant and capable of generating codes which are shared and understood between the performers, audience and host community. The dance has peculiar steps which define it as a war dance. The movement is usually very aggressive, indexical of a war lord prowling around for revenge. The solo dance by the priest around the shrine is a sign of optimum respect and homage to the late hero (*or girinya*). Here, the priest carries a sharp machete in one hand and the sheath in the other. He does a solo and solemn dance round the shrine, picking and dropping short sticks from the top of the shrine to the ground. He does this movement five times and on the sixth round, he collects a chicken and as he rounds the shrine, he beheads the chicken and sprinkles the blood on the shrine (Fig 6).

Fig. 6 The chief priest doing a solo dance, round the shrine

Apart from serving as a mark of honour to the dead warrior, this scene also signifies transition, authority and dexterity; here the right of performance is shifted to a living son, brother or relation. As the priest beheads the chicken, possible successors, who are placed strategically around the arena (in most cases the warrior's children), struggle over the head and whoever picks it automatically succeeds the warrior. In the event that the head is picked by a member of the audience, the family members will pay a fine to retrieve it from such a person. Also, if picked by one who is not interested in the dance, he hands it over to a willing brother or relation for a token. It is also noteworthy to mention that some expertise is displayed by the priest, where a particular person is favoured to succeed the dead warrior. The hen is beheaded in such a way that the head falls closest to such a candidate.

Costume is also a sign code which facilitates aesthetic beauty and exudes meaning as well as interprets mood, situation and/or events. Tiv people use a variety of costumes at different times to express and enhance their identity. Though costumes do not speak, they communicate. Most of such costumes are culturally bound in such a way that, when wrongly used, contradict perception and meaning. For instance, "*Godo*" and "*Gbagir*" are traditional outfits which symbolize tragedy (most specifically, death). If, therefore, one decides to use these materials as fashionable wears, then a lot of confusion is to be expected by people of the community; the psychological and mental fitness of such a person is rendered suspect. This is because, ordinarily, these fabrics are used to bury the dead only, not to be worn as fashionable textiles around. Perhaps, in *Girinya* dance, as postulated by Pever-Ge (1985:106);

The costuming of the dance reflects mainly masculine qualities. The head-dress is usually made up of the feathers of a bird-'Swande', only for the men with strong hearts and rare to find, and the tiny-like structures of the porcupine (Iyugh) that are shot out for self defence, which lives mostly in the mountains and forest, and is quite difficult for hunters to kill. All these serve to enhance the masculine display that the dance calls for. The loin cloth that is usually tied has in recent times and on civil occasions usually given way to the Tiv traditional dress, 'Gbev wagh' (a dark cloth with white and black stripes) worn on the waist.

This description by Pever-Ge is the actual traditional outfit of the *Girinya* dance. But today, because of the secular infiltrations of the dance, no strict compliance is maintained in terms of what to wear. Performers these days use their personal clothes with a wrapper tied round the waist as earlier mentioned. However, it could be inferred from Pever-Ge's submission that costume in this dance is a signifying code that helps to define the nature of the dance – masculinity as well as an armour of belligerence.

Sign language is a crucial aspect of the second stage of the performance, where individual warriors come out to do their dances. Here the whole story of the warriors' escapades and track record of achievement is narrated using movement. The pointing of the machete east and west is a sign indicating the period of action (from sun rise to sun set) "I went out in defence of my fatherland". He then holds out a number of fingers to both the drummer and the audience and goes into doing a dance. This, however, is a sign of self-revelation. The worth of his bravery depends on the number of fingers held together. The number of fingers represents the number of human heads he has to his credit. In relation to their (dancers') status as warriors, the more number of fingers held, the more respect is accorded the dancer and the longer his music for a solo dance. Sign language, this research discovered, is very central and instrumental to the life of the Tiv man. This is because, in the course of their migration in search of fertile farmlands, they had to move from one point to another in search of fertile lands. During migration they encountered a lot of hostility. Wars were fought and in such battlefields, signs were evolved to regulate and contain battles. Sometimes it was agreed that, if you sight a man at a close range and you were not sure of him, you raise three fingers, if he did the same, then he is a comrade, but if he did not, then, he is an enemy and war justice must be done. This was so because, with rapid expansion, it was no longer possible to know every one who came in to help prosecute such wars, because different persons had gone their separate ways to settle and could only come together during crises times to help out. Such signs, however, promote cultural identity.

Another semiotic code which is a call for unity manifests itself at the instance of feeding the warriors. This meal consists of pieces of yam boiled for just some seconds, by the priest. The posture, therefore, of standing straight with hands at the back to receive the piece of yam signifies respect and attention by the hero to the event which is of immense importance to the entire community. This meal, which is usually smeared with palm oil, signifies the binding of the body and soul to a firm commitment to the basic tenets and provisions of the dance. It also demonstrates an important aspect of Tiv traditional performances, whereby what begins as a ritual goes through an intricate dramatization and culminates in the eating of a meal by all present as a sign of unity amongst the people. The warriors eat the meal on behalf of the community. The meal is therefore seen as a binding force not only for the warrior heroes, but the entire community. This is why the priest usually implores individual warriors at the instance of this meal to remain resolute in their collective resolve and determination to defend and protect the community from external aggressions.

The piece of *anger* found on top of the shrine is also significant. Apart from functioning within the scope of a theatrical performance, sign codes identified in cultural performances have very great socio-cultural relevance amongst performing communities. For instance, in almost all Tiv traditional theatres, especially dance, performers are likely to be dressed in *anger*. 'Anger', because it is a Tiv traditional outfit, is capable of conveying to the audience the background of the performers. According to Pa Aaityough Ama, an elder in Mbaduku District of Vandeikya Local Government of Benue State, the Tiv believe in the dual existence of *"Tugh"* and *"Atetan"* (Night and Day). As such, the black colour on the 'Anger' represents "Mbatsav" who usually operate in the dark and usually in the night. White, perhaps, is purely for those with clean minds. This group is those who go about their normal businesses in the afternoon and rest through the night. Therefore, the white and black colours depict these two distinct periods respectively. Through oral interviews, it was discovered that the black and white colours also represent peace and fertility respectively. Therefore, costume does not only promote cultural identity but also projects the cultural world view of the people.

Girinya performances have both meaning and significance to the warriors who perform them and the entire Tiv community;

> "Girinya exhibits an elegant imitation of aspects of human experiences through an effective combination of music, virtual mime and costumes. In fact, watching a particular performance, one will have the feeling of having gone through a satisfying dramatic experience" (Mude, 1987:9).

The horn, drum, metal gong, and empty tins are all blended to produce a harmonized musical sensation that creates some excitement in the audience. Songs are hardly rendered. The clinking noise of the empty tins is supported by the light throbbing of the drum. The elaborate facial expressions and rhythmic head nods of the dancer convey his inner feelings: feelings that have been aroused by the music and the ongoing performance. *Girinya* is not merely a dance, it is a performance which enables the Tiv man to interact with the supernatural on one hand and entertain himself on the other. The series of ritual activities that are done to set right the spirit of the dead and thus cause such a spirit to rest in peace is in its spirituality a sacred communion with the supernatural. The dance aesthetics and social performance is quite entertaining and capable of drawing a wide audience anytime and anywhere it is performed.

Social Change and the Sign System in *Girinya* Ritual Dance

Signs lend themselves to theatrical performances in Tiv society just like elsewhere, because they are an essential ensemble of economic means which make condensation and comprehension of messages possible. Theatrical performances are milestones of signification in Tiv society, and certain social beliefs form the basis on which these performances are structured and built. Indeed, the theatre mediates and reminds the Tiv people of the values of their society, being a medium of expression which, though it may not be seen to be consciously doing so by its audience, articulates their conceptual world view. Laying emphasis on the prevalence of this function in most African performances Etherton (1982:36) observes that;

> It is very difficult for someone outside the specific culture to know what he or she is looking at and listening to during a particular performance. The very style of a performance is a short hand of actual meaning which has been established jointly by artists (composers and performers) and their audiences over a period of time.

Nevertheless, the changing face and complexion of the society today has necessitated a careful cross-examination and value reorientation with a view to reconciling certain aspects of the dance with prevailing social reality. This, however, has been responsible for the strategic loss of some aspects of the dance today, irrespective of the theatrical richness of some of these aspects. For instance, the cutting of the head of a human being from an enemy camp to bury a dead warrior (member of the dance guild) has been stopped. Not so much for the fact that this was just an exercise for the sake of it, but as we earlier mentioned, the dance celebrates valour and strength. As such, a man of valour like the warrior-heroes in this dance guild should not just be buried like any ordinary man but should be accompanied on his journey to eternity with the head of an enemy. This is perhaps the semiotic construct which makes a human head necessary.

The nuclear nature of the society today does not allow for any more of such practices, not so much for its barbarism, but for the fact that, communities that practice this dance will be in perpetual communal clashes anytime somebody's head is cut for such ritual purposes. For instance, the Mbaduku and Obudu communities of Benue and Cross River States respectively are constantly engaged in communal clashes over land encroachment because of lack of clearly demarcated boundaries. If, therefore, any of such communities find the corpse of a beheaded brother, the number one and primary suspect will be the enemy community - hence, war. Also, from the perspective of a civilized society, chopping off a fellow man's head just to bury the dead is despicable and horrible. With this realization at the back of our minds, this aspect of the dance has now been shelved and rather, old skulls are used today to bury dead warrior heroes.

The changes which came with colonialism affected tremendously the quality of performance, redefining the values and cherished ideals of such performances. Its scope today includes essentially and especially the European world view or concept of civilization. In this guise the semiotic enterprise has also changed without necessarily phasing out archaic elements. For instance, the initial costume made into skirt with raffia leaves has in recent times, as earlier mentioned by Pever-Ge, given way to contemporary textile wrappers. This, no doubt, makes appearance more aesthetic and contemporary, but has eroded the traditionalism of local creativity and fabric. With the establishment and institutionalization of the church, such performances considered "pagan" practices are fast losing relevance and value. For instance, an average Christian Tiv man finds it difficult to accommodate or be part of the *Girinya* dance. As such he or she is not willing to allow for the ritual performance of this dance if he loses his father or relation who is a member of this dance guild. If this persists, what will become of the performance in the nearest future when they (performers) are no longer living? This certainly is a question that must be addressed with utmost dispatch if we are to avert the near extinct status of most traditional performances. Lamenting also the fate of most embattled cultures, Bodley (1982:103) submits that;

> While these actions are in themselves certain to bring about profound 'acculturation', the almost total transformation of tribal cultures is assured when these actions are combined to eliminate all unique aspects of tribal culture and to bring about their full integration with civilization.

With the changing face in the process of signification, it is not unlikely that new performance forms, stemming from the changing world view, would emerge to replace old practices.

Socio-Cultural Relevance of the *Girinya* Ritual Dance

As a socio-cultural practice, *Girinya* dance is a traditional exhibition of pride, honour, unity and a corporate demonstration of valour and conquest. Usually when warriors return victoriously from wars, they assemble themselves in performance and celebration to the victory. The community through her representatives shower encomiums and chants of blessings and reverence on such young, powerful and, determined youths who had made them proud. This dance thus serves as a defence unit of the community and because of the community ties, the entire community serve as custodians of this guild. As such, during performances, especially at the burial of fallen hero chiefs and local leaders, all grace such performances. To the warriors who may have lost their lives in action (at the war front) also, this performance significantly serves as a means for the community to appreciate their effort and cause them to rest in peace.

Just as we had mentioned earlier, *Girinya* as a performance serves to cleanse the land of guilt, stains and evil deeds. The blood of the beheaded goat symbolically serves to cleanse the community as the goat is taken to mean sacrifice for the ancestors and guardians of the land. This is why, after the goat has been slaughtered, the priest does a solo movement around the arena. While this movement is going on, members of the audience are not allowed to nod in appreciation, but stand rooted and erect in one place. The value here is not in appreciation of the quality of dance by the priest but a fixed posture of respect and homage to the ancestors while the priest through movement and music communicates with these ancestors. At the end of the dance, the priest sprinkles some water on all present to absolve and protect those who may have blundered unknowingly into nodding in appreciation. Culturally, therefore, cleansing the society is relevant in re-establishing closer ties with forces that provide, protect and preserve values necessary for growth and development.

The celebrative segment of the dance is an elegant exhibition of joy, strength and conquest. It is also a show of the defeat of the threat from surrounding enemies, as this aspect can only be performed when there is relative peace in the land. Victory from a just concluded war may spur this performance during celebrative moods of Christmas, Independence Day Celebrations and other National holidays/celebrations. On a general note, once this performance is done, it is understood that the land has gained absolute peace and stability.

Girinya dance through its modes of signification has also greatly helped project the Tiv nation and has not left in doubt the strength and valour of the Tiv man. The vigorous dance steps, the wild jerking around and the furrowing eyes all jointly combine to give value and interpretation to the war-like qualities of the performers. The brandishing of the machete around the arena of performance is also expressive of the consequences should one venture to dare such a person. Perhaps, to comprehend the signs and signifying systems in this performance one needs to study them as factors in social process which have significant relation with time and given circumstances. As such, signs and symbols having been crafted carefully from the quantum of experiences a people go through, it is perhaps the entire story of the people that is told through these performances, and must be taken with a deeper sense of appreciation. From his discovery in this method of enquiry, Turner (1967:20) writes that;

> The symbol becomes associated with human interests, purposes, ends, and means whether these are explicitly formulated or have to be inferred from the observed behavior.

Within the realms of the people's cherished values and ideals, the *Girinya* ritual dance presents a spectrum fascinating enough to appeal to the people both aesthetically and culturally; it is also expressive of social norms and values. It is equally noteworthy to mention that, *girinya* in performance for a dead warrior who had distinguished himself in war and had several heads to his credit is to placate his soul to rest in peace and not come out to commit atrocities for the living. It is a celebration of his belligerency and valour. Thus, in Tivland, dance or theatre performances in general perform a number of social, political, economic and religious functions that bear a direct relationship to the general character and life styles of the people, embodying in its many artistic folds, the aspiration, yearnings, norms, values and customs of the people.

Conclusion

This work is thus a conscious attempt to dig up the hidden treasures of traditional theatre in Africa and present such treasures to a wider public and the theatre world in particular and on this premise hope that the work will lead to a rejuvenation of interest in traditional theatre and reawaken a consciousness towards this direction. African traditional theatre within the purview of this analysis was found to be rich as it adds up to a sumptuous theatre experience that requires further exploration for a fuller appreciation. The conclusion reached is that signs and signification are an integral aspect of African traditional performances that do not only enhance performance interpretation, but also offer an *entré* into the cultural values of the ordinary African.

Signifying Systems in Traditional African Theatre Aesthetics

Fig. 7: A prospective warrior picking up the head of the hen preparatory to succeeding his dead father

fig. 8: A cross section of traditional rulers in Mbaduka District of Vandeikya Local Government during the burial of a dead warrior - hero.

References

Agber, Kwaghkondo (1994). "European Commercial Enterprise and Underdevelopment in Tivland, 1900-1960", Ph.D. Thesis, University of Jos.

Ballad, J. A. (1971). Quoted in Iyo. J.E.A (1990) "The Tiv Nationalism and some Aspects of British Rule, 1854-1960", Ph. D Thesis, University of Calabar.

Bodley, John H. (1982). *Victims of Progress:* California: MayField Publishing Company.

Bur, Asom (1993). In Philip T. Ahire (ed) *Tiv in Contemporary Nigeria*, Samaru-Zaria. The Standard Writers Organization.

Etherton, Michael (1982). *The Development of African Drama.* London: Hutchinson University Library for Africa.

Gbilekaa, Saint (2006). "Preface in *Traditional Theatre in Perspective*" by Gowon Ama Doki. Makurdi. Aboki Publishers.

Hagher, I. H. (1993)."The Role of Dance in Tiv Culture" *Nigeria Magazine.* Vol.55.

Hawkes, Terence (1977). *Structuralism and Semiotics.* London: Methuen.

Mude, Iortyom (1987). "The Nature, Content and Aesthetic Values of Tiv Traditional Performances. A Paper Presented at the Seminar on Literature in Northern Nigeria. Bayero University, Kano 2nd -5th August.

Ogbonna, Charles (1991). "Drama as Human Communication" *Theatre Forum.* Vol. 1.

Pever-Ge, C. A. (1985) "Policies and Principles of Indigenous Theatre Management in Nigeria. A Case Study of Four Tiv Theatre Troupes". M. A. Project Essay submitted to the Department of Theatre Arts, University of Ibadan.

Shittu, Abimbola Robert (2003). Socio-Semiotics of Selected Contemporary Nigerian Dramatic Texts. A Ph. D. Thesis submitted to the Department of Modern European Languages, Faculty of Arts, University of Ilorin.

Thomas, D. W. (1978). Semiotics2. Communication in Man and Beast, Lexington, Massachusetts: Xerox.

Traore, Bakary, (1972). *The Black African Theatre and Its Social Functions* (Trans, Dapo Adelugba). Ibadan: Ibadan University Press.

Turner, Victor (1967). *The Forest of Symbols.* Ithaca: Cornell University Press.

Wa Thiong'o, Ngugi; *Barrel of a Pen, Repression in Neo-colonial Kenya*, Quoted in Pever-Ge (1985). Polices and Principles of Indigenous Theatre Management in Nigeria. A Case Study of Four Tiv Theatre Troupes. M. A. Project Essay submitted to the Department of Theatre Arts, University of Ibadan.

African Performance Review

APR

Annual Subscription Rates

Companies/orgs./institutions: £120
(including access to the online editions)
Online only £100

Individuals: online and Print: £50
Online only: £30

To contribute, contact the journal's editor;

The Editor, (Dr Osita Okagbue)
Department of Drama, Goldsmiths, University of London,
SE14 6NW United Kingdom. Tel: +44 (0)207 919-7581.
Email: AfTA@gold.ac.uk.

Subscription enquiries,
please contact: sales@adonis-abbey.com

Adonis & Abbey Publishers Ltd
P.O. Box 43418,
London
SE11 4XZ
United Kingdom
Tel.: +44 (0) 2077938893

Subscribe to
African Renaissance

Subscription rates:

Companies/orgs./institutions:	£250 pa (6 issues)
Individuals (UK and Europe)	£120 pa (6 issues)
Individuals (Rest of the World)	£150 pa (6 issues)
Retail sales	£19.95 (plus p&p)

African Journal of Business and Economic Research

AJBER

Annual Subscription Rates

Companies/orgs./institutions: £200
(including access to the online editions)
Online only £180

Individuals: online and Print: £60
Individuals: Online only: £30

For subscription and advertisement enquiries contact:
sales@adonis-abbey.com
Phone: +44 (0) 20 7793 8893

To contribute, please contact:
Dr John Kuada at:
kuada@business.aau.dk

Adonis & Abbey Publishers Ltd
P.O. Box 43418,
London
SE11 4XZ
United Kingdom

Review of Nigerian Affairs

RoNA

Annual Subscription Rates

Companies/orgs./institutions: £50
(online only)

Individuals: Online only: £30

To contribute, contact the journal's editor;

The Editor, (Dr Jideofor Adibe)
editor@adonis-abbey.com

Subscription enquiries
please contact: sales@adonis-abbey.com

Adonis & Abbey Publishers Ltd
P.O. Box 43418,
London
SE11 4XZ
United Kingdom
Tel.: +44 (0) 2077938893

Trauma and the Art of Dramatizing History: A Study of Soyinka's *Madmen and Specialists*

Osita C. Ezenwanebe
Department of Creative Arts,
Faculty of Arts, University of Lagos, Nigeria

Abstract

The literature of any nation is a key to unlock its past, view its present and have an insight into its future. This is because there is an intricate relationship between art and life. Theatre, among other arts, responds more promptly to social issues and events. History is therefore a viable subject matter for drama. The playwright as a social and psychological being is alive to the issues and events, which impinge on his personality and helps to form his conception of the world. This paper evaluates the complex relations of history, psychology and drama. The aim is to critically examine how the playwright demonstrates the influences of traumatic historical experiences as seen in the way he represents them on the stage. The paper proposes that: traumatic history rarely escapes the creative impulse; traumatic experiences shapes a playwright's view of the world and; this can be seen in the dramatic works informed by such events and experiences.

To further the above arguments, Wole Soyinka's *Madmen and Specialists*, a play on the Nigerian Civil War 1967—1970, which is also his personal response to it, is analysed to unravel the relationship between the dramaturgy and the experience. Other relevant materials like his novel *The Man Died*, a record of his prison experiences as a result of his role in the war, will also be analysed.

Introduction: History and the Artist

On the periphery, art and history seem unrelated since they inhabit two different worlds: the world of reality and that of illusion. However, the two worlds are not parallel; they intermingle. Fact is the basis of history; fiction that of art. Humans are the great link between history and art. They inhabit the factual world and create the fictional world by the powers of the imagination. Plato, one of the oldest art critics is quick to discover the relatedness of the two worlds. He sees the relationship in a bad light, believing that what humans create out of the real world is capable of having a destabilizing or subversive effect on the real world. He suggests that the artist, the creator of the world of illusion, be driven out of the then emergent civil society. (see *The Republic* Part Ten)

History has been a favoured subject matter of art, especially drama. Great dramatists like Euripides, Sophocles, Shakespeare, Shaw, Miller, Soyinka, etc. have recreated history on stage. Life is the meeting point of history and drama. History broadly defined as the factual life, and drama as its (life's) re-enactment. The artist's concern with history is focused on its effect on man and his environment, because Humanism in art is concerned with studies that promote man and his environment; and this study of mankind is an attitude that tends to exalt the human element or stress the importance of human interests as opposed to the supernatural, divine elements. It is therefore human interest that is of concern to many dramatists who recreate history. When Soyinka takes up the issue of the Nigerian civil war of 1967 – 1970, it is the human condition that is upper most in his mind.

The Nigerian civil war, popularly known as the "Biafran War" is history. It is an unfortunate misfortune that befalls the nation merely seven years after its formal independence. The war that broke out in Nigeria between July 1967 and January 1970 is seen by many as the culmination of the numerous crises rocking the nation before and after independence. According to Momoh (2000), there are both remote and immediate causes of the war. The remote causes he says include the imbalance in the entity known as Nigeria created by colonial administrators and the ethnicisation of the politics that precedes 1964 General Election. The immediate causes of the war are as numerous and varied as there are political and social crises.

The war brought untold hardships to the citizenry. There was blood birth, human carnage and wanton destruction of properties. Torture becomes commonplace and casualties mounts as military and autocrats swell their powers in vagrant abuses of all sorts. Corpses litter high ways and bushes. The agony of the three years of the civil war will remain in the consciousness of those who experienced it.

War is a major source of trauma, and psychologists classify it as a stressor of high magnitude. Taylor (1999), Lazarus (1968), Folkman (1984), Westen (1996) and other psychologists locate trauma within the horrors of man's experiences in the environment among which war is an outstanding example. According to them, the effect of war trauma can linger for years long after its experience, resulting in what in psychology is popularly known as Post Traumatic Stress Disorder (PTSD) with symptoms like "nightmares, flash back to the traumatic events, depression, anxiety and intrusive thoughts about the experiences" (Westen, 1996:431).

Soyinka's personal experiences of the civil war is nothing but traumatic. During the war, he has visited the then Biafran secessionist leadership in order to realise the interventionist objectives of their group "Third Force" which among others is to try to avert war by neutralising the leadership of both the federal power and that of the secessionist. His humanist action is seen as treason and that earned long period of incarceration in goal throughout the war period. His prison life affords him an opportunity to see through the evil machinations of autocracy especially in such an anarchic period such as war. His experiences at the hands of the federal powers and the inhumanities he witnesses in prison are recreated in *The Man Died: Prison Notes.* (1988). Though he learns to adapt to the monotony of his early prison life of "read-stroll-read-eat-read-sleep" (Soyinka, 1988:69), he fails to adapt to the flagrant abuse of power by security agents and the inhuman treatment of suspects. Soyinka describes the block where war prisoners are kept as being special: "it is loaded with rotting, decaying humanity" (97). There, Soyinka experiences the trauma of witnessing the agony of Biafran prisoners. Painfully, he watches the dissolution of 60 Biafran prisoners who shared the same block with him. The sixty prisoners are crammed in a small cell made for half the number. They hardly wash their clothes. They defecate in pails inside the cell even in daytime; the cell is poorly ventilated, and the cell gates are opened 30 minutes daily for the inmates to appear on a locked corridor for fresh air. Sometimes the gates he says are not opened for a whole day, and often the days they are opened, the tap is dry. Food is slid to them through the bars. Their food, Soyinka says, consists of "Bowl of weevils" in the name of beans, "a soggy dough of "farina" and a lifeless incurable diseased that went by the name of stew" (104). As one of the solders bares his body to Soyinka, he notices some kind of fungus all over his skin, "a green and yellow fungus which spread like a contagious plague all over the body" (105). And since the young Biafran prisoner has just come out from one of the numerous agonising interrogations, the whole body is peeled: "A back of purulent sores, there was no skin at all. It was a mass of sores" (106). Night and day the screaming of the tortured reaches him in his cell. There is no rest for him. Soyinka tries and establishes contact with them and is more and more intimated with the horrors and atrocities being carried out by a group of men who take laws into their hands.

Despite "the smell of rotting flesh that wafts from within those cells", Soyinka becomes more determined than ever to use everything within his thin disposal to fight, to expose and to condemn reckless and wanton human waste and degradation, and more importantly, to strengthen the will and morale of the prisoners and other suspects. Though the loneliness of "the black days of impenetrable darkness" plunges him into despair, he resolves to fight on; for "The sight of another suffering being creates an instant demand on one's own strength, deadens for the moment at least the anxiety of one's private situation" (58). The federalists see him as dangerous and contagious because of his relationship with the prisoners and his attempt to reconnect with the outside world. He is taken to

Kaduna Prison and put in the Crypt where he shares his life with "a plague of mosquitoes… "fat as blue bottles … their dark laden bellies instantly suggestive…of filth and corrupting flesh and excrement" (129). The crypt, described by Soyinka as "a torture chamber" is "a punishment cell" where punishments ranging from "water treatment", "the batten session" and others are used to force out confession from convicts and to crack their will.

Though he employs every tactics to resist the cracking of his will, he finds it more difficult to adjust to the inhumanities around him; of helpless civilians being crushed under heavy boots. Even from the dept of his enclosure, he hears "the cries of souls in torment, the wail of flagellants, wolverine howls in the dead of night, mumbled dialogue with unseen spirit visitors, the mad cackle of hyenas" (135). At one such restless night, the groans and the anguish of a man at the end of his life drive the message of human agony right into his secluded private shell. The wailing shook the walls and continuing till daybreak with no solace coming from anywhere, even when the inmates, maddened by the groans, reacted. "The bloodless inhuman steadiness of this sound of human suffering", Soyinka says, "is the most unnerving aspect of it all" (200).

The stench from battered humanity makes Soyinka to move closer to the inmates and the guards at every available opportunity, and he learns from them the greater acts of inhumanity being perpetrated in prison – the executioner's strategies for doing away with condemned prisoners and other forms of human massacre. Soyinka renews his combative spirit, toughens his will and his resistance to make sure that his mind is not completely broken. He renews his protest and his fight to alert the outside world. The more he succeeds the more the agents of the federal military might limit his freedom. He is accused of "holding classes and teaching subversive philosophies" (276). Not even the promise of release deters him, for "In any people that submit willingly to the daily humiliation of fear", he says, "the man died" (15). The more he is crushed, the more he resolves to let the world know the condition of human life in Nigeria during the war. He is convinced that "The first step towards the dethronement of terror is the deflation of its hypocritical self-righteousness" (15), and this he resolves to do both in and out of prison. Not satisfied with his humanist activities in prison, Soyinka continues the deflation in his play, Madmen and Specialists.

Soyinka's Art of Dramatising Trauma in *Madmen and Specialists*

Madmen and Specialists can be best described as a drama of trauma, an aesthetic recreation or fictionalization of horrific experiences that are buried alive in one's sub-consciousness. Prior to his arrest and detention during the war, he had been suspicious of rot within the citadel of power.

His personal experiences of harassment, oppressive interrogation and incarceration coupled with the horrendous atrocities witnessed in prison crystallise the dept of human degradation and abuse by men in power, and as Joe Orton says (concerning his inspiration for writing his play *Loot (1967)*), "The old whore society lifted up her skirts and the stench was pretty foul." (in Bigsby, 1982: 20).

Maddened by these realizations which smoulders within him like burning embers, Soyinka decides to give vent to them so as to relieve himself of their excruciating pain by writing and dramatising them. *The Man Died, Kongi's Harvest* (1967), *Season of Anomy* (1973) and *Madmen and Specialists* embody the heat of his rage, and hence are Soyinka's personal strategy for coping with the traumatic experiences. Jeyifo (2004) in his study of Soyinka's works situates *Madmen and Specialists* within the "middle, period" of his writing career, the 1970s and 1980s, which he refers to accurately as "the post civil war, post incarceration period" (Jeyifo, 2004: 89), and hence marks a turning point in his writing by becoming more sardonic, aggressively ferocious and generally more pessimistic and gloomy. *Madmen and Specialists* is a play on the evils of war and its effects on people. The context of the play is the Nigerian civil war in particular (being written a year after the end of the war) and all wars in general.

The war has just ended and Dr. Bero, the antagonist in the play, returns. Before the play starts, Old Man, Dr. Bero's father and the protagonist in the play who goes to the war front to protest in his own way, the wanton waste of human lives, has been certified mad and kept in solitary confinement in Dr. Bero's surgery under the surveillance of the Mendicants (the causalities of war). In Dr. Bero's absence, his sister, Si Bero, has employed the services of the "Earth Mothers", Iya Agba and Iya Mate, two women skilled in the use of herbs, to assist her keep his brother Dr. Bero safe in the war. The two women welcome her within their cult but at a great price of human life. But when Dr. Bero, a medical doctor turned an army intelligence officer, meets his sister on his return, he refuses to dialogue with the "Earth Mothers" and even holds them in contempt. The Mothers decides to take what they consider as their due for their work – Dr. Bero's life.

Throughout the play, the Mendicants re-enacts the philosophy and method of 'As', the new cult of inhumanity which the Old Man has taught them during the time he is doing recuperative work among them at the war front. It is in one of those rehearsals, where the old man, surrounded by the Mendicants, decides to practise the method of As on Cripple; to excise the 'tic' in the heretic in order to taste "what makes the heretic tick" that brings the play to a sudden end as Dr. Bero shoots the old man, his father, in a fit of anger. It is humanity, represented by the Old Man, who is sacrificed at the altar of "As".

The greatness of the play *Madmen and Specialists* does not lie in its content, for there is no linear action, but in the tortuous knot of its dramatic form, language and style. With the magnitude of man's inhumanity to man which he recreates, Soyinka sets out in search of the appropriate dramatic method capable of unearthing the brutal experiences in all its rawness and stamping them in the minds of his audience thereby relieving himself of their excruciating impact. This is what Jeyifo refers to as "the imperative of appropriate response" (Jeyifo, 2004:120). In an interview with John Agetua (2001), Soyinka divulges the new method of his protest theatre when he says:

> a book, if necessary, should be a hammer, a hand grenade which you detonate under a stagnant way of looking at the world ... we haven't begun actually using words to punch holes inside people ... But let's do our best to use words and style when we have the opportunity, to arrest the ears of normally complacent people; we must make sure we explode something inside them which is a parallel of the sordidness which they ignore outside" (in Jeyifo, 2001: 37 – 38).

This study explores how Soyinka succeeds or otherwise in arresting the attention of his audience by exploding in their ear, his personal traumatic experiences which parallel what they try to put up with and collapse under in the society. These explosive methods will be examined in the levels of dramatic form 9the pattern of incidents), characterization and language.

The Dramatic Form and Technique: Text and Subtext

Madmen and Specialists is a plot less play. The play defiles the mimetic mode in terms of linearity of incidents or dramatic action and borders on supra-realism which has been variously characterised as absurdist, impressionist, expressionist and the like. This study provides a basis for understanding the fragmented and seemingly illogical action in the play by evaluating the play as a drama of "brutal realism" with elliptical style or technique. Obi Maduakor explains the elliptical tradition as one in which "the artist tends to play hide and seek with the reader. The game distorts chronology, forestalls organic development of character, and relies instead on fragmenting revelation of expository details, with juxtaposition and counterpoint superseding narrative logic" (1996: 197).

In *Madman and Specialist* the incidents are arranged in line with the two worlds in which the characters move – the immediate world of the play in which they move and act, and the deep psychological world where the traumatic experiences of the real world is buried alive in their subconscious. The immediate world of the play is a post war world, a war at which the characters have fought and returned with mangled bodies but an alert mind; a war front at which both Dr. Bero and the Old Man have taught them different lessons about life. In the world of the play, the characters try to make sense of the lessons learnt from war. There is also the psychological world of their personal lives. This is the world of the subconscious reality where the pains of history: shelling, torture, deprivations and incarcerations of all sorts- lie in wait for the slightest stimuli from the external world. The characters in their physical form, being the only link between these two worlds, bestride them, and sway from one world to another at the slightest stimulation. Hence, like the famous "Abiku" or "Ogbanje" (spirit child) they belong neither completely to the dramatic world nor to that of their psychological inner being. Like 'Abiku' too, born to die and die only to be reborn, they engage in a perpetual action of coming and going. And because of the fluidity of the passage, the characters slip in and out of the two worlds unannounced, simultaneously re-enacting the subconscious world while inhabiting the social cum material in a dovetail manner. "Flashbacks" as Maduakor keenly observes, "intrude themselves on the audiences not as memories but rather as immediately realized action" (Maduakor, 1996: 198). This movement from past consciousness to the present one is "the movement of transition" – a popular mytho-poeic concept in Soyinka's writing which describes a movement from the world of the ancestors, the Great Forbearers (past, death) to those of the Living (present) and the Unborn (Future); a movement clearly dramatized in *Death and the King's Horseman*. The so-called "verbal theatrics" (236) or verbal gimmickry (240) of the Mendicants can be explained in the light of the above reality, for the action the Mendicants throughout the play is patterned in that mode, a fact that they are victims of Post Traumatic Stress Disorder (PTSD). They re-experience the trauma, and since the trauma of war is action-oriented, the mendicants act it out within the immediate action of the play.

A good example is when Si Bero reminds the Mendicants of the method of sorting the herbs. The words denoting the different methods of sorting herbs are quickly linked with those employed by their torturers to dehumanise them. Immediately they re-enact the torturer's method by playing on the semantic association of the words of herb-sorting and those used by their torturers. Words of torture and pain fill the air as they relive the experiences in the drama that ensues:

Goyi:	First the roots
Cripple:	Then peel the backs
Aafaa:	Slice the stalks
Cripple:	Squeeze out the pulps
Goyi:	Pick the seeds
Aafaa:	Break the pods. Crack the plaster
Cripple:	probe the wound or it will never heal.
Blind Man:	Cut off one root to save the other
Aafaa:	Cauterize
Cripple:	Quick-quick-quick, amputate!
	(Blind Man lets out a loud groan)

Goyi:	Cut his vocal chords
Aafaa:	Before we operate we cut the vocal cords
Si Bero:	Have you all gone mad? (20)

For Si Bero, the Mendicants are mad because she does not understand the way their minds are going. She is outside the experience they are relieving. What the characters relive above is akin to Soyinka's experiences of the prisoners. The phrase "peel the back", for example, reminds one of the thrashed Biafran prisoners at the Kirikiri Maximum Prison which Soyinka described in *The Man Died*. The play is a parody of life. Similar parody of Dr. Bero's practice at the end of the play takes a tragic dimension as Dr. Bero shoots his father in outrage. Most of the words have double meaning. Beneath what is said, a lot is being said.

The play replete with such examples as the one above; for example, the Mendicant's re-enactment of mock-trial sessions in an "As" system; the process of aggressive interrogation by which Dr. Bero elicits truth from suspected offenders or rebels, etc. Devoid of the psychological subtext, incidents in the text may appear as "macabre games reminiscent of horror films" (Angya, 2005: 133) with the characters, the Mendicants "playing along with the Old Man" and merely "re-enacting the mental and intellectual thinking which he (the Old Man) has released to them" (Angya, 2005:134).

But up and above Angya's superficial observation, the action of the Old Man is beyond a mere forcing down of his ideology on his apostles, that is, indoctrinating them with the philosophy of "As". This would rather mean another form of brutality, albeit an academic/intellectual one. Rather, the Old Man (the alter ego of Soyinka) and the Mendicants are best seen as brothers in the experience of traumatic. The Old Man's philosophy of "As" only help to open the eyes of the Mendicants to the reality of the traumatic experiences smouldering their subconscious. 'As' then acts as the key that frees them from its continued enslavement. They are quick to learn the Old Man's philosophy and pit holes with those of their oppressors because they have learnt from their personal experiences the hollowness and brutality of Dr. Bero's practicality and "Scientifism". The psychological subtext provides the basis for understanding only a segment of the relationship between the Old Man and the Mendicants; for as Jeyifo writes:

> An entire monograph could be written on the nature of the spiritual and psychic inter-subjectivity which binds the mendicants to the Old Man and aligns them to his frenzied evangelization against 'As' and its "priesthood", 'gospellers" and "enforcement agencies" (2004: 153)

Such is the richness of Soyinka's work and the multifaceted nature of his dramaturgy seen also in his use of characterisation as a technique.

Characterisation: the Battered Humanity in the Battle of Essence

Madmen and Specialists has been rightly described as a drama of ideas in which the ideas appear to be more important to the dramatist than the characters. Hence, characters are submerged in the ideology and its explication. They become character types or archetypal, symbolic figures used by the dramatist to drive home the message of his argument. In re-creating the trauma of his experiences, Soyinka chooses psychotic and psychologically imbalanced characters in whose life the impact of such brutality is evident. All the characters in the play are diseased either in body or mind or both.

As a whole, they constitute a throng of battered humanity whose self is divulged from its essence, and whose action is a continuous effort to unite their battered self to its original whole that is its essence. From Dr. Bero, we learn that the Mendicants are those wounded during the war. They are the convalescents among whom Old Man works to help them physically adjust to life where they could. They are therefore the victims of war, in whom the trauma of war leaves its physical, psychological and emotional marks. CRIPPLE walks with his buttocks or clutches, Blind Man finds his way with his stick, Goyi is a limbless one, a mass of flesh "held stiffly in a stooping posture by a contraption which is just visible above his collar" (Soyinka 1971:7). Aafaa suffers "St. Vitus Spasms". The Mendicants live with Post Traumatic Stress Disorder (PTSD) and constantly relive the traumatic experiences of the war throughout the play. They are the footstools of As; and as Soyinka writes in the opening poem of his play *Kongi's Harvest* (1967), they are "the rooted bark, spurned/when the tree swells its pot;/ the mucus that is snorted out/when Kongi's (military dictatorship) new race blows" (Soyinka 1967:1). Like Soyinka, the Old Man sadly observes the effects of war: "War brutalises the human soul", for "it's strange how these disasters bring out the very best in man – and the worst sometimes (Soyinka, 1971: 20).

A good example of the impact of traumatic experience on one's psychology can be illustrated with Aafaa's explanation of the origin of his spasms:

> They told me up there when it began, that it was something psy-cho-lo-gi-cal. Something to do with all the things happening around me, and the narrow escape I had ... (Soyinka, 54).

There are so much evil both in the experiences of the characters and in the world of the play. "We heard terrible things. So much evil" Si Bero complains (Soyinka, 30).

Soyinka is very much concerned about the health of the human mind. According to him, the human mind is the house of reason and intellect, and hence, the seat of revolutionary change. No matter how mangled a man's body is, Soyinka believes that a sound, thinking mind which thinks aright, can lift the body up from its stupor. He makes this view clear in an interview with Harry Kreisler (1998) in his analysis of the relationship between theatre and revolution, when he says:

> I believe implicitly that any work of art, which opens out the horizons of the human mind, the human intellect is by its very nature a force for change, a medium for change. It has been used to help the black man ... work out his historical experience and literally purge himself at the altar of self realization ... the other revolutionary use... has to do very simply with opening up the sensibilities of black man ... towards very profound and fundamental truths of his origin that are in Africa.... This for me this is revolutionary (Kreisler, 1998: 7).

In the play Soyinka creates his alter ego in the Old Man who like Professor in Soyinka's *The Road* possesses exceptional mastery of the resources of language with which he fights the status quo so as to liberate the human minds of the Mendicants from total collapse. With his cult of a dramatic conceit "As", Old Man launches a linguistic warfare against all forms of inhumanity and their political apologists in order to expose the inherent absurdity and violence within them. For example, when Aafaa mentions the word "electric", the Old Man drifts into the world of torture and the instruments of torture to expose its vicious mechanisms as he says, "Electrocutes, Electric Chair. Electrodes on the nerve centers – your favourite pastimes?" (He asks Dr. Bero, an 'As' apostle) (66)

Unable to endure the continued subversion of the political system, the agents of "As" certify him (Old Man) mad. But the question is "Who are the Madmen and who are the Specialists in this play?"

An understanding of the two worlds of the play in which the characters move throws much light on the question. Literarily, on the level of the immediate world of the play, the Old Man and his cohorts (the Mendicants) are the madmen while Dr. Bero and the agents of military autocracy are the specialists. The Old Man with the cult of mysteries around him, often speaking in a manner that is out of place with the immediate environment, can be seen as being "mad". After all, what he says is incomprehensible to the military autocrats and their agents. Worse still, his flagrant disregard of the limits of the duty assigned to him in the war front makes the authority certify him as mad. Dr. Bero, Old Man's duty

> Was to help the wounded readjust to the pieces and Remnants of their bodies. Physically. Teach them to make baskets if they still have fingers. To use their mouth to ply needles if they had none, or use it to sing if their vocal cords had not been shot away. Teach to amuse themselves, make something of themselves. Instead he began to teach to think, THINK! Can you picture a more treacherous deed than to place a working mind in a mangled body? (37).

Surely it is only a mad man that can dare the orders of the Political "As".

To literally-minded audience too, Old Man's logical proposition of cannibalism as a way of managing wastes in human flesh at the war front is nothing but the product of a lunatic mind. Similarly, the Mendicants, in their fractured piece and pieces that goes for a body; their begging antics often carried out with music improvised with knick, and knacks exhibit credible signs of madness. In addition to their unkempt physical condition is the manner in which they vitiate from one world to another. Their utterances, which sound so incoherent and nonsensical on the surface, are taken as visible signs of an unmistakable madness. In the exchanges between them and Dr. Bero, they all plead insanity:

> Dr. Bero: ... Would you call yourself sane?
> Aafaa: certainly not, Sir.
> Dr. Bero: You got off lightly, why?
> Aafaa: I pleaded insanity.
> Dr. Bero: Who made you insane?
> Aafaa: (...). The Old Man, Sir. He said things, he said things. My mind ... I beg your pardon Sir, the thing I called my mind, well, was no longer there (37).

The mad Old Man is too daring to replace Aafaa's former enslaved mind with a critical one that asks question. Their one major offence is therefore the attempt to have a thinking mind in their mangled body – an offense of no less magnitude to subversion. Old Man, their ring-leader, seen as suffering from an infectious disease, is aptly put in solitary confinement. His disease Dr. Bero says is "mind sickness".

Dr. Bero and other military autocrats in this way of literal reasoning are the Specialists. His training as a medical doctor and later an army intelligence officer needs no doubt as to the soundness of his mind. His professional decorum and precision easily go off as a sound mind in a sound body. The expertise with which he carries out his duty is parodied by the Mendicants:

> Cripple: Him a dutiful son? You're crazy (referring to Goyi)
> Blind Man: I know what he means (He points an imaginary gun) Bang! All in the name of duty (11).

On the other hand, if viewed from the psychological subtext of man's inhumanity to man, Dr. Bero and the apologists of military autocracy are the Madmen while the Old Man and to an extent the Mendicants are the Specialists. Who else can be more insane than one, like Dr. Bero, who abandons his humanitarian job of saving life to one of reckless abuse of life and torture of those he is trained to save? Or, which sane human being can throw filial bond to the wind and brutalise his father to the extent of shooting him dead all in the defense of one's philosophy? Which mentally stable medical doctor can give a scientific approval to cannibalism and make human flesh in war front his daily meal, and even returns home loaded with it after the war? These are actions only of a monster in a human form, not even a mad man. In the same vein of reasoning, Old Man, who as the vision and voice of his age and people, sees through the wickedness of the political 'As', and refuses to keep quiet but rather stakes his life in awakening his people to the ironic mask of inhumanity, is the Specialist. Old Man is a Specialist of double rank: a Specialist in radical unmasking of brutality in the garment of generosity, duty and patriotism; and a Specialist in enthroning human dignity and freedom.

The above logic only proves the rich subtext of Soyinka's play and the fluidity of the characters. *Madmen and Specialists* is a drama of elaborate symbols in plot, character and language.

The Language of Absurdity and the Absurdity of Language

As with form and characterization, the "radical discontinuities and disjuncture" which Jeyifo identifies in the play (Jeyifo, 2004 :143-144), "the art of double talk pointed out by Maduakor (1996: 236), "the somewhat confusing use of flashback scenes" complained by Martin Esslin (in Beier ed., 1979: 288) can be better understood with a close reference to the bi-partite form of the incidence. To be able to simultaneously present the two worlds, Soyinka uses the appropriate metaphorical language of parody, double entendre, pun and paradox with which the characters mimic and satirise one world while inhabiting the other. This creates a mood of ironic, cryptic humour and radical cynicism. This subversive language helps the characters to, in the words of Jones, "change back and forth continually" (Jones, 1973:106) between the two worlds. An example is the following dialogue between Dr. Bero and his father the Old Man in which the Old Man twists the words "smoke" and "suffocate" to serve his satire of Political 'As':

Dr. Bero:	Or smoke you out. You will suffocate, slowly.
Old Man:	Smoke. Smoke-screen. That's what it all is.
Dr. Bero:	What?
Old Man:	The pious pronouncements, manifestos. Charades. At the bottom of it all humanity choking in silence (62)

As Old Man twists the words "smoke" and "suffocate" to serve his subconscious world, Dr. Bero is lost. What? He asks. He fails to follow Old Man's logic because both inhabit different worlds of experiences. This however is not so with the Mendicants who understand the Old Man's logic and imbibe it completely and not only utter but act it out. Asking questions like "Who are the cyst in the system" that irritates? (73), immediately unravels the density of Soyinka's language. The word "As" is the most sustained verbal conceit. It represents all forms of inhumanity, autocracy and brutality in nature and life. With it the Old Man determines to match and counter the illogicality inherent in all inhuman systems with its own absurdity.

Among all the techniques of language, the most outstanding is the use of dry, ironic humour with which Soyinka make a sick joke on the inhumanities of war. This masks anger at its peak. The playwright often makes cynical comments even on issues that are very dear to him. The issue of cannibalism is dramatised in dry ironic humour. "We've got to legalise cannibalism", says the Old Man. "I'm going to try and persuade these fools not to waste all that meat". "After all, all intelligent animals kill only for food". (And since man is an intelligent animal, he should eat what he hunts down). Dr. Bero attests to the success of Old Man's mission. The perpetrators of inhumanity and human carnage have actually started eating the meat of those they kill. No need for wastage. Dr. Bero confirms this fact to his sister: "I give you the personal word of a scientist. Human flesh is delicious. Of course, not all parts of the body. I prefer the balls myself" (35). Soyinka uses these cynical comments to elicit gut response by deliberately becoming provocatively outrageous. This detached cynicism makes the play difficult to understand. In Adejare's *Language and Style in Soyinka* (1992), the author opines that Old Man's crime for which he is branded insane and incarcerated is because he is teaching the Mendicants and officers to eat human flesh. This is a gross misunderstanding of the play based on two factors: the misunderstanding of Soyinka's dry, ironic humour and the failure to relate the play to the rich psychological subtext of Soyinka's prison experiences during the war which he is dramatising. Language remains Soyinka's greatest achievement in this play.

Conclusion

Soyinka successfully combines the drama of purgation and liberation in this protest theatre. The "Atunda" consciousness, an ancient Yoruba mythology signifying constructive rebellion, is celebrated as a subtle way of igniting the revolution that works, by first infusing the minds of the people with radical thought meant to free them from their broken, wounded state so that they can have the sound mind and body necessary for a political action. Maduagwu in his essay "The Atunda Consciousness and Constructive rebellion in Wole Soyinka Socio-Political Vision", gives a clarion call that "The new Atunda consciousness should pierce the heart of men to ignite action" (Maduagwu, 2004: 510) just as the Old Man ignite the minds of the Mendicants. It is against this phenomenon that Adeoti (2006) and Obafemi (2004) still foresee hope in Soyinka's seemingly pessimistic drama. Obafemi opines that there is light of hope since "The mendicants, representative of society, have been given the power to think. Si Bero still has gained knowledge of the healing herbs. There is still hope, yet, even though Bero is the one holding the gun", (in Angya, 2005: 142-143).

Works Cited

Adejare, O. (1992) *Language and Style in Soyinka: A Systemic Textlingustic Study of a Literary Idiolect*. Ibadan: Heinemann Educational Books.

Adeoti Gbemisola and Evwierhoma, Mabel (eds.) (2006). *After the Nobel Prize: Reflections on African Literature, Governance and Development*. Lagos: Association of Nigerian Authors (ANA).

Angya, C.A. (2005). "Will there be Peace? Images of War and Brutality in Wole Soyinka's *Madmen and Specialists*", *Nigerian Theatre Journal: a Journal of the Society of Nigerian Theatre Artistes*. Lagos. Vol. 8, No 1. (pp. 132 – 145).

Bigsby, Christopher (1982). *Joe Orton*. London: Methuen.

Durand, V.M. and Barlow, H.D. (1997) *Abnormal Psychology: An Introduction*. New York: Brook and Cole.

Esslin, Martin (1979). "Two Nigerian Playwrights: Wole Soyinka and J.P. Clark" in Beier, Ulli (ed.). *Introduction to African Literature: An Anthology of Critical Writing*, London: Longman.

Folkman, S. (1984). *Stress: Appraisal and Coping*, New York: Springer.

Jeyifo, Biodun (ed.) (2001) *Communications with Wole Soyinka*. Jackson MI: University Press of Mississippi.

Jeyifo, Biodun(2004) *Wole Soyinka: Politics, Poetics and Postcolonialism* Cambridge Studies on African and Caribbean Literature. Cambridge: University Press.

Jones, E.D. (1973) *The Writing of Wole Soyinka* (revised edition). London: Heinemann.

Lazarus R.S. (1968) "Emotion and Adaptation: Conceptual and Empirical Relations". W. Arnold (ed.), *Nebraska Symposium on Motivation*, Lincoln: University of Nebraska Press, (pp. 175-266)

Lazarus, R and Folkman, S (1984). "Coping and adaptation" in W.D. Gentry (ed.), *The Handbook of Behavioural Medicine*, New York: Guilford Press.

Maduakor, Obi (1996). *Wole Soyinka: an Introduction to his Writing*. Ibadan: Heinemann.

Plato, (1955), *The Republic*, H.D.Lee (trans.) London: Penguin Books

Soyinka, Wole (1967). *Kongi's Harvest*, London: Oxford University Press.

Soyinka, Wole (1971). *Madmen and Specialists*, Ibadan: University of Ibadan Press.

Soyinka, Wole (1988). *The Man Died: Prison Notes*, Ibadan: Spectrum Books.

Soyinka, Wole Interview with Harry Kreisler in "Topical Excerpts from interviews with Wole Soyinka", *Stanford Presidential Lectures in the Humanities and Arts*

http://prelectur.standford.edu/lectures/soyinka/soyon.html//theatre 3rd March, 2007. (Pp. 1—7)

Taylor, S.E. (1999). *Health Psychology*, (4th ed.), Boston: McGraw-Hill.

Westen, D (1996). *Psychology*: *Mind, Brain and Culture*, New York: John Wiley and Sons.

Environmental Impact Assessment and the Dramatist: A Conceptual Study of Esiaba Irobi's *Hangmen Also Die*

Norbert Oyibo Eze
Department of Theatre Arts
University of Nigeria, Nsukka, Nigeria

Abstract

The subject of Niger Delta predicament and crisis has been the theme of many editorials and publications in Nigeria and elsewhere. Before the November 10, 1995 execution of Saro-Wiwa and other Ogoni environmental activists, for their collective resolve to address certain fundamental interests that affect their common identity and humanity, Esiaba Irobi had, in a spine-chilling tragedy, *Hangmen Also Die*, painted bizarre and horrifying picture of this society, which is in acute danger of socio-economic and ecological extinction as a result of terrible effect of oil exploitation.

In this paper, attempt is made to examine *Hangmen Also Die* as an impact assessment study. It is the position of the paper that the Niger Delta youths represented in the play as the 'suicide squad', are victims of neglect and peripheral attention, and that as a social class, they turned deviants in order to draw urgent attention to a zone, which supplies the wealth of the nation, but which is in sore state of economic and social development. It is argued that in this play, Irobi demonstrates unreservedly, "the daring involved in naked confrontation with adversaries".

Introduction

The Nigerian environment constitutes the major theme of the dramatic writings of Esiaba Irobi. Indeed, many of his plays reflect the poor state of power relations in the country, as well its socio-economic impact on the people. However, Irobi's plays, especially *Hangmen Also Die*, appear very disconcerting to some critics, because "an element of nihilism unavoidably creeps into the picture" (Maanem and Bennis, 1979:3). For example, Toni

Duruaku observes that:

> Irobi manages to present protagonists who rise above despair, even though their choice is not praise worthy. Therefore, they will at worst generate anger for their base option (2000:105).

The reason for the above comment is not far to seek. *Hangmen Also Die* undoubtedly vitalizes certain "instincts that people don't like to gratify except with the help of ingenious disguises and a rather childish hypocrisy"(Fraser, 1976:10). According to Freser, "these instincts, which are most deeply rooted in the human psyche, are on the one hand, fear, and on the other, the taste for blood and death" (10).

Nonetheless, a general resentment of these instincts does not obliterate them from reality. There are conditions where human beings often prefer death to life. It is the position of this paper that the protagonists of *Hangmen Also Die* have touched that limit. In this article, attempt is made to demonstrate that this explosive play does not benumb our moral faculty. Rather, it is viewed as a hyper-intensive response to the challenges arising from poor implementation of Environmental Impact Assessment vis-à-vis oil exploration in the Niger Delta, as well as the unhealthy political climate in the country.

Environmental Impact Assessment

According to Uche Okpoko, "the field we now refer to as Social Impact Assessment (SIA) or Environmental Impact Assessment (EIA) emerged in response to the United States' National Environmental Policy Act (NEPA) of 1969, which took effect in 1970 (2004:91). Okpoko cites Freudenburg as positing that this environmental act is necessitated by "the society's increased concern with environmental degradation, and the social implications of technology" (91). Environmental Impact Assessment, therefore, deals with policy-guidelines on how to regulate and/or ameliorate the frightening and materialistic havoc of technology. This is imperative because technology now appears to over-determine where and how we live, as well as our basic health conditions. Herbert fill argues that "technological development has drifted since its beginning, advancing not so much to foster true human progress as to perpetuate" (1974:61) physical and mental breakdown. EIA is "anticipatory and should give planners useful information for selecting an alternative in the light of economic, social or security implications of human actions" (Okpoko, 2004:91).

To pay lip service to the global concern on environmental degradation due to human actions on the natural environment, Nigeria established Federal Protection and Environmental Agency (FEPA) in 1988. FEPA is charged with the responsibility of restoring, maintaining and enhancing the ecosystem and ecological processes essential for the functioning of the biosphere. The policy equally spells out guidelines for safeguarding fishes, forests and wildlife, as well as modalities for the establishment of certain infrastructural facilities to mitigate the hazardous effects of toxic emission, and solid wastes. However, Okpoko argues that "Nigeria's environmental arrangements are good in principle, but poor in practice" (2004:105). For him, "the only lessons Nigeria learned from the United States appear to be in procedural and legal provisions for the implementation of EIA/ SIA" (105). He concludes that the enforcement of the provisions in Nigeria is found wanting in many respects (105). Okpoko's assertions above are quite correct because:

> Since the discovery of oil at Oloibiri more than four decades ago, the Niger Deltan people have continued to watch helplessly as some multinational oil firms despoil their land, water and aquatic lives. This damage of the people's traditional means of livelihood has brought untoward economic, as well as socio-cultural and psychological hardships upon the people (2004:106)

However, the degradation of the natural habitat of the Niger Delta people is used in the play as a metaphor for the apparent decay and crises that bedevil Nigerian political landscape. Indeed, what the playwright attacks vehemently in the play is the politics of self-aggrandisement, which creates a disturbing gap between the Nigerian people and their aspirations. As it is in the play, the Nigerian youths are the most affected group in the unhealthy power relations in the country. Sound education no longer guarantees employment for them. This makes them feel unwanted. The agony of being alienated from one's own country compelled Irobi and many of his contemporaries to flee from Nigeria. In a brief bio-data placed on the Internet, Irobi is described thus, "Esiaba Irobi was born in the Republic of Biafra and has lived in exile in Nigeria, Britain and USA". The playwright's denunciation of Nigerian citizenship is a reflection of his total rejection of the unhealthy power relations in Nigeria. His identification with Biafra is significant in two ways. Firstly, even though Republic of Biafra is utopian, Irobi believes that it is better to dwell in an utopian world than to live in Nigeria and suffer socio- economic and political hardships, as well as anguish of the soul. Secondly, Biafra is a symbol of rebellion. And rebellion against the status quo is the hallmark of Irobi's dramaturgy. Through *Hangmen Also Die*, the playwright attempts to incite the Nigerian youths to pick up arms against their uncaring leaders.

Synopsis of *Hangmen Also Die*

Hangman Also Die, which is set in the oil rich Niger Delta, is compartmentalized into six phases. In phase one, it is hanging day for condemned prisoners," but Yekini, the male convicts' hangman refuses to do his job. He finds it difficult to hang the youths, whom he feels are right in murdering Chief Erekosima for embezzling the money given to their community in compensation for the oil spillage that destroyed their land.

In phase two, members of the suicide squad are already toughened into brutes by the traumatizing condition of years of joblessness. They double both as assassins and thieves because they believe that to live without jobs is to live a lifeless life. In phase three, these unemployed youths argue that there is a thief in all of us, and that the thief "creeps out when the plague of poverty and hunger falls upon the land like a blanket of darkness" (p.46). In phase four, Tamara, a very strong and powerful priestess and teacher, stumbles on the group in their bush-hideout and convinces them on the need to recover the compensation money from Chief Erekosima. In phase five, the suicide squad disrupts the ceremony, where Erokosima is to be crowned the Amatamaso 1 of Izon state, and gets the Chief kidnapped. In phase six, the boys are apprehended for hanging Chief Erekosima when he refused to surrender the remainder of the compensation money. In phase seven, we are back again in the prison yard as in phase one. Yekini is sacked for refusing to hang the boys. Ekpenyong, the female convicts' hangman, is used to dispatch the youths to the beyond.

Hangmen Also Die as an Impact Assessment Study

Elsewhere, this writer argues that, "in its articulation of now an actual historical phenomenon, which at its period of composition and publication (*Hangmen Also Die* was first staged and published in 1989) had remained a secret to history, *Hangmen Also Die* is most prophetic" (2000:35).

Hangmen Also Die is eminently prophetic, not only because its action, in actuality, has been paralleled by the hanging of the Ogoni environmental activists, led by Ken Saro Wiwa, in November 10, 1995, but also because it foreshadows the current youths' restiveness in the Niger Delta, due to the continual degradation of their natural environment by oil firms, and government's poor implementation of the provisions of Environmental Impact Assessment in respect to oil exploitation in the region.

In the first place, one of the measures, which ought to be taken to assuage the anger of a people whose land and traditional means of livelihood have been destroyed would be to guarantee them an alternative source of employment. But, as the play indicates, this is not to be. In spite of their sound degrees, the youths remain knights without shinning armour. Their encounter with the Directorate for Employment speaks eloquently about their frustrated attempt to engage themselves in worthwhile means of livelihood:

R.I.P: Seven years later, we met again. This time at the office of the

Directorate for Employment---which claims that the government is giving loans to the unemployed graduates who want assistance for self-employment for small-scale industries.

> ACID: We were there seven times a week.
> R.I.P: From eight in the morning to eight in the night.
> DAYAN: We even went on Sundays.
> ACID: But we never got a kobo.
> R.I.P: So, there, on the corridor of the Directorate for Employment, we remembered Dr.Oghansiegbe's speech on the uses of terrorism (p.30).

The problem of joblessness is quite excruciating, and this triggers off in the handicapped youths, a feeling of worthlessness. According to Eze:

The suicide squad is a child of depravity, a child of necessity, formed as a means of walking out of the terrains of neglect, poverty and futurelessness. The members of the squad do not merely want to exist, they want to live, and living means having all the paraphernalia of living, namely, good jobs that can assist them to build their own houses, marry and, therefore, bear children (2000:34).

Maanem and Bennis express the view that "feeling such as love, hate, honor, envy, pride, anger, elation, warmth, shame and sorrow are fundamental, not peripheral to the understanding of interpersonal dynamics" (1979:2). This implies that it is difficult to "amputate feelings from the study of social life" (2). In spite of their talents, the members of the suicide squad are tossed into the social heap of nothingness by the same society that expects so much from them. The group's acts of vandalism, violence and crime, which produce psychic fear, should be seen as normal behavior expected of a desperate people in society. Though crime and violence are reprehensible acts, they are, in certain conditions, the only palpable means of protest. I think that in their violent disposition, the suicide squad wants to be seen as a contagious disease so that immediate effort can be made to procure remedy.

The idea of unleashing terror on the presumably innocent people is to cause a major psychological shift, to force other people to feel themselves, their own kind of fear and anguish, and to compel the government to realize that they are leaders of victims. In examining the protagonist of John Osborne's *Look Back in Anger*, which is analogous to Irobi's protagonists in *Hangmen Also Die*, David H. Karrafalt argues that:

If the condition of despair in which the individual finds himself is accompanied by the discovery that he is alone in recognising the degree of man's failure, and alone in feeling the pain of this recognition, then the possibility appears a way out of both isolation and the despair. This possibility is to have others recognize the same kind of pain (1970:80).

This is exactly what the suicide squad seeks to achieve through its numerous harassment and thieving activities. Fraser argues that "an intuitive sympathy only occurs when one believes that one knows with reasonable precision, how the victim is himself perceiving and judging what is happening to him" (1979:59).

Furthermore, Chief Erekosima's saga in *Hangmen Also Die*, represents a clear manifestation of the oil firms' hypocrisy and lack of genuine consultation with the communities in their interest and desires. Almost all initiatives are paternalistic and generally initiated from the outsider perspective (Okpoko, 2004:107).

Instead of dealing with the people's representatives, oil firms often relate directly with government officials, who are usually not interested in the affairs of the masses. The play suggests that Chief Isokipiri Erekosima belongs to a royal family, the family of "the great King Pepple of Bonny" (p.75), who in the past had maintained control in the Delta province. Like most Nigerian politicians, Erekosima gets into both civilian and military regimes through royal influence, not mainly as a result of his people's choice. This is the reason he does not see politics as an institution for responsibility, or care for the welfare of the people. When Tamara reminds him that "a great man is he who drinks with kings and still maintains the common touch" (p.86), he promptly replies:

> I prefer to maintain touch only with kings and rich men. I don't want to be soiled by the filth of poverty. My own greatness is different. It does not tolerate meddling with the creatures of the swamp: the crabs, the mudskippers, the periwinkles (p.86).

The foregoing underscores the tragedy inherent in the Nigerian political environment. While the leaders themselves consider poverty as a contagious disease, and flee from it by all means, they encourage its widespread among the common folk through mass rooting of public funds and squandermania mentality.

Chief Erekosima is a symbol of cancerous leadership that has continued to plague Nigerian politics. Through him, the playwright paints disquieting picture of Nigerian leaders, "the type of people they are, their life-style, values and the type of image they create for the people" (Okolo, 1994:82). His coronation with the public money indicates that like a typical Nigerian politician, Erekosima does not conceive power as service to the people, but a great opportunity for self-aggrandisement and financial showmanship. Through him, Irobi depicts the Nigerian politician as a brute Machiavellian, who does not see any relationship between politics and morality. As it has been demonstrated by many Nigerian leaders, and succinctly expressed by Erekosima:

> Politics is an art of what is possible. It is an art of survival. Personal survival. Morality does not come into it (p.85).

In *Hangmen Also Die*, Irobi juxtaposes the ostentatious life-style of Chief Erekosima with the plight of Ibiaye, the blind beggar, in order to palpably reveal the huge gap between the "self-possessed and the dispossessed" of the land. Even with stolen money, Erekosima wants to be made a deity, but Ibiaye who lost all he has to the spillage, including his sight, is seen as a disembodied entity to be pushed to the street, to suffer and grope for food. Of course, Ibiaye symbolizes ordinary Nigerians whose honesty and hard work hardly pay any dividends. His presence at the coronation scene demonstrates how the helpless masses often resort to the humiliating tendency of feeding from the crumbs under their oppressors' table. Ibiaye is fully aware of Erekosima's untoward behaviour. He realizes that "someone is reaping where he did not sow" (p.67), but the necessity to stay alive compels him to attend the coronation ceremony. Hear him out:

> I who once fed people, I am now fed. And why else would I be here? If not to find some crumbs for my empty stomach. Why else would I be here, at this festival of foolishness, if not for this little one (p.71).

The death of the youths in the play paints the true picture of the kind of measure, which the government has been taking to "assuage the justifiable indignation of the youth in the Niger Delta" (Osakwe, 2002:10). In the words of Jimor Osakwe, "all we hear and read from the media is about enlarging, training, arming and compensating the security forces to contain, maim, and kill the protesting youths" (2002:10). Although the establishment appears to have won in the play, Osakwe rightly argues that as far as the Niger Delta conflict is concerned, the:

> murderous orientation and approach by the government cannot provide a reasonable solution to the crisis. It is the usual predatory, piratical, capitalist and imperialist disposition to the plight of innocent, weak, exploited, dehumanized and humiliated people who are struggling for their birth, social and economic right (2002'10).

Osakwe rightly suggests "that the enormous financial resource allocated to training, arming and compensating the security personnel is more than enough to train and equip the same personnel to create sufficient condition favourable to the social-economic advancement of Nigerian youths throughout the country" (10).

Realizing the objective of Environmental Impact Assessment depends largely on adequate attention being paid to the plight and welfare of the masses, whose daily living depends on the natural resources around them, which are constantly dissipated. But from Ibiaye's experience, which is similar to what the masses pass through daily in the Niger Delta, we observe problems of displacement, shortage of food supply, poor state of drinking water and acute problem of accommodation. Worst still, people whose health is impaired often do not have adequate and nearby hospitals for prompt medical attention.

From the analysis above, this writer agrees with Laing and Cooper that "ambiguous facts are evident when we view a person from different perspectives with different conceptual frameworks" (1971:18). If the protagonists of *Hangmen Also Die* are examined from the perspective of criminal psychology, we will certainly see despicable beings who have crossed the boundary between the human and the monstrous. But if, on the other hand, they are viewed from the perspective of frustration-aggression theory, we will see normal human beings, who are psychically deeply wounded, because their "future projects" appear to leave them "forever short of fulfillment" (Roth and Sontage, 1988:203). It is this feeling of unfulfilment, this blockage of goal-oriented effort that makes the suicide squad never to be at rest, but to risk their lives in dangerous activities. Hegel argues that "It is by risking life that freedom is attained," and that "the individual who has not staked his life, may no doubt, be recognized as a person" (1901/1967:223). It is, therefore, to give eloquent testimony to the primacy of feeling that Irobi created the suicide squad. His aim is, at least, to paint an authentic picture of civilization and its discontent. Today, the youths' restiveness in the Niger Delta, which *Hangmen Also Die* foreshadows, is a clear sign of the people's bitterness about the poor implementation of the provisions of Environmental Impact Assessment *vis-a vis* oil exploration and exploitation in that area, as well as a painful state of socio-economic and political affairs in the whole country.

Conclusion

In this paper, the writer argues that *Hangmen Also Die* does not benumb our moral faculty, as some critics would want us to believe. It is argued that the play dramatizes certain philosophical truth about man's existence, and that is, that man hates constraints, and can do anything to liberate himself. G.W.F. Hegel posits that any condition that chains man and makes it impossible for him to actualize himself, is a "violent ordinance of the world, and that any means employed to resist it is justified, so long as the goal is to do away with the suffering it brings about"(1901/1967:393). Irobi does not merely juggle up ideas about constraints and resistance, he allows them to issue forth in action. It is the writer's view that *Hangmen Also Die* is an impact assessment study, a hyper-intensive reaction to the negative effect of oil technology in the Niger Delta.

More importantly it is argued in this article that Irobi utilizes the situation in the Niger Delta as a platform to launch an attack on the Nigerian leaders, whose conception of power as an art of personal survival, put the Nigerian people in deep socio-economic and political mess. This writer is of the view that the playwright's anger as expressed in the play, is in place. Irobi, no doubt, knows that "the Nigerian, like everyone else, can think, invent or discover something worthwhile if he has sufficient rewarding incentives for his toil; if, for instance, he has public recognition and respect for his effort; above all, if through his thinking and discoveries, he can adequately feed himself and his family" (Okolo,

1994:94). But *Hangmen Also Die* suggests that poor incarnation of values by the Nigerian leaders renders Nigerian intellects and their talents impotent, and oftentimes, turns vibrant youths deviants.

List of Works Cited

Duruaku, A.B.C. "Esiaba Irobi's *Hangmen Also Die*: Artistic Exploration or Didactic impulse". *Okike: An African Journal of New Writing* No. 46, October 2000.

Eze, Norbert Oyibo. "Meaning and Significance in Esiaba Irobi's *Nwokedi* and *Hangmen Also Die*." *Okike: African Journal writing* No. 44, February 2000.

Fill, J. Herbert. *The Mental Breakdown of A Nation*. New York: New View Points, A Division of Franklin Watts inc., 1974.

Fraser, John. *Violence in the Arts*. Cambridge: Cambridge University Press, 1976.

Hegel, G. W.F. *The Phenomenology of Mind*. Trans. J. B. Baillie. New York: Harper and Row publishers, 1901/1967.

Irobi, Esiaba. *Hangmen Also Die.* Enugu: ABIC Books and Equipment ltd., 1989.

Karrafalt, David H. "The social Theme in Osborne's plays." *Modern Drama* Vol. Xiii, No. 1, 1970.

Laing, R.D. and D.G. Cooper. *Reason and violence: A Discourse on Sartre's Philosophy 1950-1960. New York:* Pantheon Book, 1971.

Maanem, John Van and Warren Bennis. "Introduction." *Essays in Interpersonal Dynamics*. Ed. Warren Bennis, John Van Maanem, Edgar H. Schein and Fred I. Steele. Homewood, Illinois: The Dorsey Press, 1979.

Okolo Chukwudum B. SQUANDERMANIA MENTALITY: Reflections On Nigerian Culture. Nsukka: University Trust Publishers, 1994.

Okpoko, Pat Uche. "Environmental Impact Assessment and Development Decision-Making in Nigeria: Lessons from the U.S." *African Journal of American Studies* Vol.1, No.1, 2004.

Osakwe, Jimor. *Justice and The Niger Delta Crises: Historical Analysis in Political and Socio- Economic Philosophy*. Benin City: NP., 2002.

Roth, John K. and Fredrick Sontage. *The Question of Philosophy*. Belmont, California: Wadsworth Publishing company, 1988.

http://www.finearts.ohio.edu/theater/faculty.and.staff/esiabairobi/htm

Feminist Aesthetics in African Theatre of the Colonial Period

Esiaba Irobi PhD
University of Ohio, Athens, Ohio, USA

....women... armed and unarmed, afire with courage and enthusiasm, then flung themselves in successive waves of compact masses upon the districts where the settler, the soldier ...held sway. ...Villages and airports were frequently attacked...But it must be added that thousands...were mown down by colonialist machine guns.
- Frantz Fanon *The Wretched of the Earth*

Nobody can make you feel inferior except with your consent.
- Eleanor Roosevelt

You strike a Woman? You strike a Rock!
- Indigenous South African feminist slogan

The Vagina also has Teeth.
- An Igbo Proverb.

Introduction

In the months of November and December, 1929, fifty women were shot dead in several towns in South-Eastern Nigeria by the British colonial administration. They were shot for protesting against a poll-tax about to be levied upon them all the way from London as part of the English imperial intelligence of making the natives pay for their own colonization (see Said, 1994, Rodney, 1981, Young, 1990 and Fanon, 1967). My grandmother, Danne Akwarandu, was one of the forty thousand Igbo women who participated in this revolution. On the evening of November 29, 1929, she came home with the stains of the blood of some of the slaughtered women on her dress.

Before the fifty women were shot dead - and another fifty wounded – they had inflicted maximum damage on the economic and administrative infrastructures of the colonial administration. More than ten thousand strong, the women - known collectively as *oha ndom* - attacked government roads built through forced labour; they attacked British-owned cars, trucks, railroad stations, fences surrounding public areas, mercantile buildings: GB Ollivant, African Trading Company, Niger Company, African & Eastern Company, Barclays Bank, United Africa Company, factories and warehouses that housed palm oil and other commodities for export, native court buildings, colonial administrative headquarters and jails. The women tore at the very fabric of buildings with their fingers and the weight of their bodies – in some cases breaking down not only the doors but whole walls. They blocked the roads and railways with their bodies (see Bastian in Allman, Geiger & Musisi, 2002). They lay on the rail road tracks ready to be killed for their political convictions. Here is an eye witness account which underscores the immense meta-theatricality of the revolution. It is by an English expatriate, Mr Logius, who worked for the G.B. Ollivant merchandise company in Aba. He had left his house at about 9 am in his car and suddenly near the level crossing gate he found a big crowd of women about two hundred in number. Some were actually lying on the iron railings on the level crossing of the railway:

> I had to stop my car because the suburban train left that station to go down to Port Harcourt. The women would not clear the crossing. The driver [of the train] made many attempts to pass through, but they remained there. Then the train driver returned back to the station. The women then surrounded my car and danced about and they were very excited. They had heavy sticks and some were carrying bricks. I kept a smiling face and was pleasant to them. They wanted to shake hands with me, so I did so. Then one of them tried to knock my helmet off. Another woman broke the windscreen of the car. They became very wild. My driver asked me to leave the car as he said they would do me harm. I left the car and endeavored to return to the French Company's bungalow but the women would not let me pass. I went to the African & Eastern Company's bungalow and the women rushed to the bungalow. Afterwards I joined my car again and on the way *I met other women who mishandled me* (italics mine). Eventually I reached my shop. (PRO LO583/176/8:34-60)

The revolution which the British colonial administration labeled "riots" was widespread and very well organized. The "demonstrations" which involved thousands of women, stretched from Oloko, forty miles North of Aba to Opobo fifteen miles south of Aba, a radius of about sixty miles. They were so well-planned and orchestrated that even the British colonial officers attest not only to their efficient organization but more significantly their economic and political imperative. For example, Mr Ferguson, an English District Officer stationed at Owerri, a town forty miles, north-west of Aba, was two or three miles away [to] the Okpala Native Court – about twenty miles north of Aba - when he noticed, on 9th December, a crowd of women walking along the road and singing. Most of them were each carrying a young palm frond either in their hands or about their persons. On inquiry, he learnt that they were going to Owerrinta to hold a meeting of protest against the taxing of women. "They were perfectly orderly and he managed to turn some of them back" (34-60). Ferguson, then, narrates that by about 2 pm, the women had returned from Owerrinta and this time they had managed to get hold of sticks. They rushed into the [Okpala] Native Court compound and proceeded to batter various buildings. With the aid of a few Court Messengers and an odd labourer or two, Mr Ferguson succeeded in driving them out of the compound but, as he puts it,

> it was impossible to keep them out...it was obvious that they were *not* going to listen to what I said. They went round beating buildings, and having done their little piece they retired and danced about.... This went on all afternoon. At about 5:30 pm the last band of women appeared....they started throwing sticks about. They tried to pull down the [Okpala] Native Court and I endeavoured to stop them, but they made a rush and pulled down the one small building. That was all the damage done. They quietened down after that ...but their demands were impossible...*The first demand was that women should not be taxed. The second was that the price of [palm] produce should go up at once and the price of imported articles should go down. The third was that the tax on men should be reduced and they gave reasons why these things should be done. Obviously I could not promise them any reduction on male tax....they only asked for reduction at first. Two days later they changed that to the abolition of all tax* (emphasis mine)....Some of them may have mentioned it but I cannot recall any definite statement that they wanted to drive away the Warrant Chiefs....They all kept saying they were `Ohandun', (sic) that is to say `women of all towns'(34-60).

This tradition of African women enforcing political change, en masse, and by any means necessary, is not peculiar to Igbo women. In fact, it is a widespread practice in most African societies and continues till date. For example, in July, 2002, thousands of Ogoni, Izon, Itsekiri, and Kalabari women in the oil-producing delta region of Nigeria confronted Chevron, Texaco, Shell BP and other American and British oil companies and demanded jobs as compensation for drilling crude oil from their land and damaging their ecology thereby making it impossible for the women to farm or fish and feed their families. These women took over the premises of the oil companies and refused to leave until their demands had been met by the foreign oil companies. When things came to a head, the women stripped naked and cursed the oil companies with the potency of their motherhood.

Several scholars have studied these revolutions, particularly the Igbo women's revolution of 1929 and 1930, from historical, sociological, anthropological, political perspectives focusing on the social and dialectical impetus to the revolutions. Some, mainly women, have adopted the events as important historical and theoretical reference points for the advancement of contemporary feminist discourse (Wangari et al in Rocheleau, 1996: 287-308; see also Calloway, 1987, Mba, 1982). What I want to do in this study is to extend or flesh out their theoretical discourses by looking at the revolution from the perspective of performance studies as a "theatrical event", a form of political theatre in which we can see a clear performance of the Igbo notion of " Oha Ndom!" i.e. the female, collective, political, force *in motion and action!* In contemporary terms "Oha Ndom" can be defined as a kind of all female political pressure group or autonomous female oppositional political party, thoroughly organized, partially hierarchic, and set in place within the Igbo indigenous system and definition of democracy to watch, critique, and where necessary, veto the excesses of the patriarchal status quo through transformative and efficacious political action.

My intention in this undertaking is to highlight how this incandescent event was made possible by a fusion of indigenous Igbo theatre/performance aesthetics and the politics that gender ideology provoked in a colonial African society at the turn of the twentieth century. I also want to use the incident to theorize African female subjectivity by allowing the women to speak in their own voices, hence the quoted narratives taken from the women's testimonies at the trials conducted by the British colonial administration after the insurrections. But before I do this let us re-examine the scholarship on the subject for greater clarity as to the historical factors that provoked the revolution.

In his book, *The Warrant Chiefs: indirect rule in Southern Nigeria* (1972), Afigbo provides a rich backdrop to the Igbo Women's revolution. He examines how the British settled down in Igbo land and ignorant of how the pre-colonial society was structured and the place and the power of women in it, rendered women invisible based on the parallel of their own country where Emily Davidson, a suffragette, had to throw herself against the King's horse or try to stop it at the Derby in 1913 – an act of martyrdom - before English women were allowed participation in English democracy, a democracy in which women had no say and could not vote until 1918.

The British, discovering that the Igbo had no centralized system of government but actually ran small scale, village-based, face-to-face, democratic polities in which collective participation – including women- was mandatory, decided to appoint Warrant Chiefs as intercessors or administrative intermediaries between the European District Officers and the Igbo communities. These Warrant Chiefs were, of course, chosen, not on the basis of their leadership qualities, intelligence or integrity, but on the basis of how much they could suck up to the white District Officers. The women detested this. Once in office, these local symbols of his majesty's foreign tyranny colluded with court interpreters/court messengers to exploit their own people in every sphere of life: judgment in the native courts, the taking of titles, tolls, levies, education of children (Afigbo, 1972: 249-295). Since the women bore the brunt of the greater portion of the extortions, discriminations and marginalization, the entire colonial system also annoyed the women. Here is a testimony by Rosanah Ogwe of Azumini as to the economic reasons why they planned the revolution:

> The Chairman (an Englishman): What do you want to say about markets? Rosanah Azumini: As regards markets, we had five markets from time immemorial and they were going well but to-day none of those markets are functioning. If articles are taken to the market for sale, Court Messengers would only throw 4 pence on the ground for an article which should fetch say, three shillings and go away with that article. If the woman resists or talks in any way about the matter she is assaulted by the Court messengers (PRO LO583/176/8: 34-60).

At this point Rachel Nenenta, a radical, articulate, hot-headed and political accomplice of Rosanah's, forced her way into the witness box of the Commission of Inquiry and corroborated the information about the widespread exploitation:

> I agree in the main with what the last witness said...Market is our main strength. It is the only trade we have. When market is spoiled, we are useless.... If you have property – it may be property you acquired yourself or property given to you by your parents or husband – and you take it to the market for sale, it is seized by Court Messengers and taken away without payment....If a woman is strong enough to catch hold of the Court messengers and say " Let us go to the Chief in order that I may report to him what you are doing, all that the Chief will say when they go to him is "Go away , I cannot do anything in the matter." You return home crying. You cannot get redress even if you take out a summons against the Court Messengers. If your case is heard in the Court and you are not satisfied with the judgment and you ask for review or appeal, the case is left for the District Officer to review. When the District Officer [British] comes to review the case, he will not ask you what you have to say in the matter but he will simply say, "Let the judgment of the Chiefs stand" (34-60).

As Nina Mba (1982) points out the colonial administration also discriminated against women in their employment of the "natives" in the colonial civil service, and even in education. Apparently, the British were more interested in training girls for the roles of mothers and wives than anything else and so the educational system privileged men who were needed to run the colony as clerks, secretaries, cooks, house servants, teachers and policemen. By 1932 when the Lagos Women's League appealed for women to be employed in the civil service, the Chief Secretary replied:

It is doubtful whether the time has arrived when women could be employed generally in the clerical service in substitution for men. In future they may be employed as telephone operators, counter clerks or book binders (quoted in Mba, 1982: 64).

It was only by 1941 that women could be employed in the Statistics section of the Custom's Department. By 1944 there were only seven African women in the clerical and technical services in Nigeria. The highest paid, as Assistant Inspector of Prices, earned ninety pounds per annum. Women were admitted into the police force only by 1955. This continued invisibility of women was not out of oversight. It was a permanent aspect of the British colonial policy. Their resistance to the inclusion of women in the colonial political family is vividly captured in a circular A16/1951 in which it is clearly indicated that "only in exceptional circumstances should a woman be considered for appointment to senior grade posts in scales F and G" (65).

Equally, Christianity, the bible-wielding, smiling branch of the colonial enterprise, via the church, had erased much of an entire culture of women's priesthoods, ritual activities and indigenous performances which gave women avenues to express their discontent with unprogressive patrilineal political policies. This erasure of their religious privileges perhaps irritated the women the most. They had lost their place and say in the running of their society in a way never before experienced and coupled with this, came the threat of a community poll tax in which the women would possibly pay the same amount of money as the men who were benefiting more from the patrilineal colonial and indigenous political system. The women decided that the excesses of tyranny was often made possible and supported by the patience of the oppressed. They decided to go to war. And they used indigenous, extremely theatrical structures, as well as songs taken from pre-colonial indigenous performance to express their outrage. Before we examine the theatrical aspect of this event, let us first hear the political testimony of a woman called Ahudi who was summoned to articulate the grievances of the women at the "Commission of Inquiry" after the women's revolution or what the British called "the riots", but which the women themselves explicitly named "ogu umunwanyi" i.e. the women's revolution or the women's war:

All the chiefs whom we ask to be deposed should be deposed, otherwise the trouble will go on. New Chiefs whom the women say are good men, such are the people we want. Chiefs take all [our] money. ... You may take evidence for many days, but unless you come to a conclusion which will satisfy the women, we will follow you everywhere. Formerly we never made demonstrations in this manner, but we do so now in order to show you that women are annoyed. If you come to a satisfactory conclusion which will satisfy the women, then peace will be restored. If not, then, we will create trouble again. No doubt, women like ourselves are in your own country. If need be we shall write to them to help us. We shall continue fighting until all the Chiefs have been got rid of, but until then the matter will not be settled. If a new man be appointed, then all the women should be present, and all the men should be present, and both should approve his appointment. (Pro Lo583/176/8: 34-60)

Here we see another often unrecorded and unacknowledged dimension to the revolution: the yearning by the women to be part of the decision-making process of their new, albeit colonized society.

There were other remote causes to the revolution and the dragon tail of terror that it produced for the British colonial administration. The taxation of men had been introduced by the British at a time of economic instability, the early 1900s. A slump in the prices of palm kernel and palm oil due to the fluctuations in the world market meant that the prices of imported goods rose. The Igbo women who were middle-women in buying palm produce locally and selling them to foreign companies at major commercial towns, Aba Owerri, Opobo, Onitsha, Okigwi, and using the money they were paid to buy imported goods such as cloth, tobacco, cigarettes, sardines, margarine, beverages, kerosene, wine and spirits from wholesale British companies - in order to retail these European goods for a little profit - were hard hit and experienced a drop in their fiscal income and their standards of living. Interestingly, the key influential women who masterminded the revolution came from this economically upscale class. Part of the agenda they put forward, which was never heeded by the colonial administration, was that the prices of palm produce should be permanently fixed just as the prices of the European goods that they bought from overseas were fixed. The less well-off women were already feeling the burden of the taxation on men since the women, being housewives, had to contribute or sometimes had to pay the taxes on behalf of their husbands, thereby depleting their already meager financial resources.

Colonial Administration and Sexual Politics

Finally, another historical factor that led to the upheaval was that some of the British District officers, as well as male Christian missionaries, were sleeping with African/Igbo men's wives and when information got round the communities, the colonialists became more tactful and discrete, preferring to have native women who lived in outhouses behind their own colonial houses and who only came in at night to teach them the Igbo language and culture. These women were called "Sleeping Dictionaries" and they were the women who, because they could read and write and could speak passable English actually gave the women all the information as to when or how to attack the European colonial institutions of oppression. Distrusting the male interpreters who often changed what the white man was saying to suit their own greedy financial needs, the "Sleeping Dictionaries" and a few other self-educated women, who attended local adult education night schools - also spoke to the white men as well as read out the women's grievances to the District Officers, point by point, before the fences came crashing down. This is how Charles Allen, a former British colonial officer, narrates this interface between power, sex and insurrection in his book, *Tales from the Dark Continent*:

> ...in the outposts most people [Europeans]...had an African girl living with them...sometimes referred to as sleeping dictionaries.... She would not have her meals with the officer, and she would not be seen in the house. She would merely have her own house behind, along with his servants and his servant's wives, and she'd only come into the house after dark. That was the life of most lonely men in the lonely stations and of course, they did learn to speak the native language far better than us who lived a life of abstinence (1979: 79).

It is interesting to note that when a secret circular admonishing colonial officers who were living in a state of concubinage with native women was issued round the colonies with accompanying threats of punishments from London, all sorts of unpleasantness befell the whole of the government service until a hurried circular B was sent round saying that the office of the Secretary of State for the Colonies will no longer take a very serious view of people living under such circumstances anymore (18). So, in thinking about the factors that led to the women's revolution we need to include the illegal colonial traffic in the sexual currency of the colonized, another layer of exploitation which had to be confronted by the women.

I will now use this historical event in Nigeria which has not been given the detailed international scholarly i.e. performance studies analysis that it deserves to foreground the centrality of women to both 'theatrical' and 'political' resistance to British imperialism in Africa from 1885-1995. I will argue that one way to avoid the postcolonial tendency of silencing subaltern subjects in the field of theatre and performance studies is to find rhetorical and representational strategies that will allow the so-called "unlettered", "uneducated," "illiterate," "subaltern," and "historically-silenced" characters to articulate their experiences and the inherent agency in their political and theatrical actions which create history in the first place.

The Role of Women in Indigenous Igbo Theatre

Unlike the USA and UK where there are no clear or easily identifiable traditions of performance created in totality by women, Igbo society flourishes with such women-created and women-centred ritual and artistic forms of expression. Igbo women have child naming ceremonies called *Onu Nwa* that they practice. At the age of ten, in my mother's compound at Owo Ahiafor, I witnessed an extremely ribald dance done at midnight in which the married women ridiculed all men, including their husbands and celebrated the superiority of their sexuality and femininity through songs, mime and sexually-ecstatic choreography. The women also play important roles in communal funeral ceremonies which are highly theatrical and are responsible for providing newly bereaved widows with entertainment and humor during their period of *igba nkpe* or mourning for their husbands. In particular, women cleanse the community of ills and clean or 'kill' the old year symbolically so that the new year can be born. They also create and choreograph dances that are uniquely theirs and which are seen publicly at great occasions within the community. These include *Nkwa Umuagbogho, Anyantolukwu, Edere, Kperembu* and many others. In the Ngwa community, women had elaborate theatrical performances such as *Owu, Mgbede, Aguumunne, Mmuolama* and participated as actual actors/characters, on equal footing with men, evident in the *Umuimo* and *Ikoro* dramatic performances.

While it is true that the masquerade form excludes women in many parts of the Igbo nation, this cannot be said with conclusive and total finality as Chinua Achebe does when he says in the foreword to the book, *Igbo Arts: Community and Cosmos* that "if the masquerade were not limited to the male sex alone, one would have called it the Igbo art form per excellence" (in Aniakor and Cole, 1984: ix). As a matter of fact, there is a tradition of women's masking in the Izzi community of North East Igboland. This masking tradition is significant in the sense that it reminds us of *functionality* as a crucial element in the creation, practice and sustenance of indigenous Igbo theatre traditions. This is the way Chike Aniakor describes the origins of *Ogbodo Enyi*:

> In 1975 children of the Izzi village group, Nkaliki, began to die from illnesses attributed to unspecified "evil spirits." Petitions presented to the community oracle, Uke, succeeded in dispelling these spirits; order between the human and supernatural realms was restored and the deaths stopped. However, in return for its intercession and patronage, the oracle, in a dream to its priestess, made an extraordinary and unique request. Uke asked Nkaliki women to organize and dance *Ogbodo enyi* in its honor. Now well-established through out Nkaliki, the women's masquerade represents a complete departure from all known Igbo (and other Nigerian) masking traditions ...that dictate all such activities as exclusively male prerogatives (ix).

It is interesting to note that this rare and unique female masking tradition mirrors or parallels the male counterparts in iconographic, sonic, proxemic, sartorial and other literacies. There is little or no difference in their semiologies. The women commission the elephant masks from a sculptor who also makes the male masks. They ask a weaver to produce a bell-shaped raffia costume. They then select leaders and learn *Ogbodo Enyi* songs, dances, and music. They make their outings at the same time as the males. As an institution, the masquerade unites women under its aegis; it is a public symbol and a celebration of their social identity and contributions to the society. Women, however, as Aniakor observes, are collectively represented by a single mask whereas the males are differentiated by hierarchical age grades which are more in number in the community.

Finally, in the Igbo nation, storytelling, practised under tree branches in the moonlight or by the fireside as evening food is being prepared in the *usekwu* (kitchen) was, until the invention of satellite television, the primary process whereby the children learnt through their mothers, the arts of public speaking, rhetoric, verbal wit, and indigenous styles of acting through the craft of re-enacting the characters in the folktales. Other moonlight verbal games such as *nkee nkaaa*, conundrums, tongue twisters, which most Igbo children learn also through their mothers reinforce that impression I have that in the Igbo nation, and perhaps across the world, women are actually the primary carriers of culture. The segment of the oral arts that children learn from their fathers is predominantly the proverbs. But the accent put on motherhood and what mothers contribute through domestic education into developing the artistic and political consciousness of the young in Igbo society is perhaps best captured in the name given to female children: Nneka, mother is supreme, reminding us all that nobody, except through DNA test in contemporary times, can tell exactly who his father is. But mother is constant. Hence the immunity Igbo society gives women within their political system as a group that sits in perpetual, watchful opposition for political excesses from the male ruling hierarchy and who have the power collectively to correct these excesses by dethroning any male ruler or leader who deviates from the moral peg or who maltreats the women as the Warrant Chiefs and District Officers came to learn to their own grief.

Theatre and Politics in Igbo Society of the Colonial Period

I will now make a connection between the ritual and performance aesthetics of indigenous Igbo theatre and the fire and force they gave to the women's revolution. I will begin by presenting a few accounts of the activities of the women during the *ogu umunwanyi* which were incontestibly not just theatrical but theatre itself since they involved role playing. Here is a description of what happened at Umuaro after the women had seized Okugo's cap and were waiting for his full trial by the colonial government. (Okugo is the Chief of Oloko who started the hysteria by counting women in his constituency during a census which prompted the meetings, plans, strategies to demolish the Warrant-Chief system and the tax.):

> At Umuaro, the women were comparatively mild...On the afternoon of the 11th December some women came to the Native Court with palm leaves and gave some to the Native Court clerk and the Chiefs as a notice that the court must be closed until their case with Okugo was finished, a proof that they still believed that the danger of the taxation of women had not passed. The following morning, hundreds of women rushed into the Native Court yard, dressed in rags with leaves tied round their heads but without sticks, and said that all the chiefs must leave or there will be trouble. *Some sat on the benches and imitated the chiefs while others pretended to be Court Messengers. Eventually they drove the chiefs out and danced and sang round the Native Court till evening* (emphasis mine). The burden of their song was that the Court clerk and messengers and all strangers should leave town. No damage was done to any building (PRO LO583/176/8: 34-60).

Here we see the efficacy of satire and parody as Hommi Bhabha suggests in his brilliant essay, "Mimicry and Man" and as Michael Taussig and Paul Stoller have expatiated in several books which deal with discourses of the colonial encounter in Africa and other parts of the world (see Bhabha, 1994). It is crucial to point out that every performative element described in this scenario above was extracted from meta-languages in Igbo rituals, ceremonies, masquerade performance and indigenous festival and ritual theatre. The palm leaves in the semiotic vocabulary of Igbo culture and theatrical sign systems are symbolic of the sacred. To put palm fronds round an object or space in Igbo culture means that the object or space has been sacralized and therefore has become sacrosanct and therefore should not be touched. Whatever has been circumscribed by the palm fronds belongs to the gods. So, by giving the clerks the palm fronds, it meant that the courts had been turned into shrines and remain, until further notice, areas where no trespass can be allowed unless the clerks and colonial administration wanted war as result of their willful violation of territory made spiritual and symbolic by the women. When the men violated the sanctity of the space, the punitive repercussions implied by the symbol of the palm frond became manifest and was translated by the women from ritual symbolism via theatrical performance into violent political action.

Dance as a Metalanguage in Igbo Theatrical and Political Performance

In virtually all eyewitness accounts of the women's revolution that we have read, we notice that dance, mime and movement were the primary vehicles for expressing the inarticulatable depths of anger and agitation that the women were feeling, motivating them to go onto the war path and to celebrate their victories. In other words they used dance, a kinesthetic literacy in Igbo theatrical semiology, for choreographing their grief, their political resolve, their triumph as well as their gender and sexuality. This means that unlike the predictable and almost banal routines on Broadway, The West End or on the BBC's Legs and Co, dance in Igbo culture is a weapon of terrifying political and artistic power. As we saw in numerous instances, the dances were signifiers of what and how the women were feeling about their oppression. They found their release, not merely of emotion, but of political intent and action though the power of dance. In many instances, dance, because it is comprised of physical movement - the body does not lie – became the semiotic signifier and the emotional graph of the political and ideological convictions of the women. In its poly-vocality, it expressed both their spiritual role in Igbo society as well as their traditional responsibility as agents of political change in the most lucid way, but one totally undecipherable to the district officers who could not understand why the police at Imo River, for example, refused to shoot at the marauding women. The native policemen, being Igbo, could decode the dance as a politically transformative message, one to be interfered with only at the risk of death. Meanwhile all the dances looked the same to the Europeans whether the women were stamping their feet on the ground or bending and mooning the white men with their buttocks.

In his book, *Performance Studies: An Introduction* (2003), Richard Schechner points out very insightfully that the spiritual and mythopoeic meta-texts encoded in dances by Africans is *realistic* to them. By this he is suggesting that the values, ideas and thoughts encoded in this gestural and limbic lexicon of physical but choreographed expressivity do not constitute some symbolic unattainable dream of faith that is beyond the realms of everyday "pepper and salt" reality i.e., some abstract thing disconnected from the business of daily living. Schechner is trying to say that the fusion of the functionality of dance with political performance and efficacy during the Aba Women's Revolution is the equivalent of what theatre goers in the West would consider psychologically realistic and believable, not an idiom that belongs to the realm of abstruse ritual.

Sitting on a Man as Indigenous Igbo Comic and Satiric Theatre

Let us now look at the theatrical styles and structures used by the women to prosecute their political agenda. The idea of "sitting on a man or a chief" is one of the most theatrical scenarios any playwright or screen play writer can scoop in his or research for a play or a film. In fact, it is the quintessence of what Bakhtin(1965) meant by the carnivaleque where by the masses use laughter, irony, humour, elements of self-parody and finally indeterminacy to lampoon the status quo or reverse the equation of who really has control of real power with a given unpredictable moment in the political and social life of a society. Women, largely of a lower social status and gender stratification, bonded by grievance, enter like a troop of actors to rehearse a very funny play that may end in the political "beheading" of the chief as in Peter Weiss' *Marat Sade*. In the context of the Aba women's revolution, sitting on a man incorporates all the elements one can imagine in a Dionysiac festival in Greece in 4 BC, plus what happens in New Orleans during Mardi Gras and the para-theatrical activities that accompany carnival in the Caribbean, especially Trinidad and Tobago. One can even argue that stick-fighting, processions, masking, and a lot of the other political symbology in African Diasporic carnival performance have their origins in African theatrical practices such as "sitting on a man" (see Okpewho *et al*, 2001).

The women having arrived in a corrupt chief's or man's compound may bring out a blackboard and begin to play the role of the man's wives by scoring his sexual performance on the blackboard with a piece of chalk, then simulating the position the man likes the best, how he heaves and sweats like a he-goat on heat and how he falls over and begins to snore after orgasm. Each little skit will be accompanied by a song. Then other aspects of his life will be parodied through mime, costumes, props and other theatrical artifacts. Every tiny mistake he's made or offence he has committed in the past will be recalled and rendered in song thereby preserving it indelibly in the community's memory and political consciousness. Meanwhile, the women will be helping themselves generously to any fruits on the trees in the man's compound, palm wine or food available, as penalty for their time that the man is wasting, by not responding quickly enough to their demands. It is usually a bawdy and ribald occasion. Speech is also used, for example, if the man stammers this is incorporated into the performance, for realistic characterization. Numerous lewd jokes are told. But in the end the comedy may end with burning down the man's house, if for example, he refuses to surrender his warrant cap to the women as a trophy of victory in their war of the sexes. Therefore, "sitting on a man" means keeping the person under house arrest and amusing themselves at that person's expense and detriment until the person meets the women's demand which will always involve some measure of indignity and reduction of the man's esteem and political power within the community. It incorporates female drag, dis-identifications, role-playing, costuming, parody, dance, mime, proverbs, witticisms, rhetoric, improvisation, processions, and comic acting of a high order. In most Igbo societies, songs are used as performative catalysts for firing up soldiers for war. Sometimes this is accompanied with dance and music. The women adopted this martial aesthetic extensively in their revolution. And so gluing it all together is the meta-language of song which I have categorized as a form of linguistic/sonic literacy which requires decoding and which most unfortunately the non-Igbo speakers or colonial officers/expatriates could not decipher. The weight or burden or implications of such songs as 'Nzogbu enyimba enyi," "What is that smell? Death is the smell?" (usually used in burial or funeral rites), "Iwe na ewe anyi Iwe, iweeeooo iwe. " (used in war) were lost on the colonial officers.

Songs as Metatexts

Perhaps, the song of the women during the Aba women's tax riots as they marched towards the colonial headquarters to strip the resident colonial officer naked, measure his penis with a wooden ruler, drag him out before burning down the building is highly representative of what I have described above as linguistic and sonic literacies from the indigenous Igbo theatre traditions.

> Oleghi nwoke turu ukaaaa
> Agbawaa ya onu amu
> Agbawa ya onu amu nike
> Agbawa ya onu amu
>
> Oleghi nwoke turu ukaaa
> Osikwa nime ohu
> Osikwa nime ohu putaaa
> Osikwa nime ohu.

This is an extremely rude song conveying the women's outrage through sarcastic sexual metaphors. It is still sung by women today when they want to get their way with the men during political disputes in some parts of Igbo land, particularly Umuahia area A very tame translation would read:

> Where is the man who made this law?
> Let's slice open his penis
> Let's slice open his penis by force
> Let's slice open his penis!
>
> Where is the man who made this law?
> Did he not come out of the vagina?
> Did he not emerge from the vaginal passage?
> Did he not come out of the vagina?

Crime, Punishment, and the Colonial Quest for the Truth

It is important to note that despite the occasional looting that accompanied the revolution, the Commission of Inquiry exonerated the women from any accusations of premeditated violence or stealing. In an impassioned reservation by V.R. Osborne, Chairman of the Commission of

Inquiry, clearly stated his understanding of the political, instead of destructive, motive behind the insurrection when he catalogued that the general intention of the women can best be gauged by briefly reviewing what had taken place immediately before the accident which occurred [at Aba] at about 10 am [on the] 11th December, 1929. In his summary he points out that two days previously, at Owerrinta (only fourteen miles from Aba) the mobs of women invaded the Native Court; the judicial caps of the Chiefs were demanded ; the Chiefs were chased into the bush; and the houses of the Court Clerk and the Court Messengers were looted. On the day prior to the accident the Assistant Commissioner of Police (Mr Matthews) travelling in a Native Administration lorry, had stones, sticks, and yams thrown at him and a six foot log of wood was placed across the road. On the same day, in an adjoining district, the Native Courts at Nguru and Ngor were destroyed; the lock ups at both places forced [open] and the prisoners released. At Ngor they pulled down and looted every building in the Court compound. At Nguru they destroyed all the buildings except the Rest-House:

> In Aba itself, on the day prior to the accident, the women had begun to parade and demonstrate in the mainstreet of the township in front of the factories. ...That evening (10th December) there was general disorder in Aba native town . ...[The} women said, "There will be more women coming along in the morning, and they would come to fight." A local chief was reported to have been flogged and Okwandu, clerk of the Native Administration gave evidence that the women in Aba that evening did say they were coming to destroy the offices and factories next day PRO LO583/176/8: 34-60).

Osborne also mentions that the sudden rush of the women to the District Office which occurred a few minutes after the accident by Dr Hunter was due to the fact of,

> the Resident's arrival... The women were most anxious to see the Resident. *As long previously as 27th November, they had sent a big deputation to Port Harcourt to present their grievances, but unfortunately he [the Resident] had not been able to see them* (34-60). (emphasis mine)

The first demand of the women at the district office in Aba, Osborne reinforced in his report, was to see the Resident and "the women in front, when he appeared, tried to quieten the remainder that they might listen to him" (34-60). With the evidence above, Osborne comes to the conclusion that the vast majority did come with the idea of doing damage as an expression of their grievances and that the damage might have been much greater had the women joined at Ekeakpara and returned with other women to Aba. In his own words: " It was absurd... to suggest that several thousand women had suddenly armed themselves with sticks, and arrayed themselves as they had done , within a few seconds, as the result of the motor accident" (34-60). As regards the destruction and looting of factories along Factory Road in Aba, Osborne states:

> Between the motor accident [Doctor Hunter's] and the looting of the factories there was in my opinion, no direct connection whatever, and *the false importance now attached to that minor incident wrongly belittles the real grievances felt by the women, and the unprecedented extent to which they were moved by them throughout so great an area* (34-60). (emphasis mine)

The political efficacy of Igbo Women's Revolution can be gauged by the radical response it provoked from the British colonial administration. The Europeans sent district officers, anthropologists, ethnographers, historians and annotators like Margery Perham and Sylvia Leith-Ross to study the Igbo political system in detail with particular attention to the role that women played in it as different from what obtained in England in the 1920s. As a result of these investigations and the books that came out of them the entire British colonial system was partially rethought and overhauled and women were given a more prominent role within the system though risible by today's standards. Particularly noteworthy is the fact that the colonial administration took more seriously the education of girls. As John Oriji, an Igbo historian puts it:

> The first Womens' revolts of 1929 was organized by rural women, while a second wave was organized from 1950- 1960 was associated with educated urban women. The revolts served as an inspiration to those who organized subsequent revolts and women's movements. Its {the revolution's} achievement include that it helped women to mobilize themselves and change the existing political order during colonialism. It enabled some of their leaders who emerged as heroines to attain a privileged status in Igbo society comparable to those of titled men and warriors. The revolt contributed to the emergence of the modern Igbo women who are currently engaged in diverse occupations. It ranks as one of the most outstanding primary resistance movement in Nigeria [Africa and the World] (1994: 19)

Conclusion

In conclusion , the presentational strategy I have adopted in this essay, namely of allowing the rebel in the subordinated to speak out for themselves is, for me, a form of interventionist discourse, what Foucault calls the silent but dangerous 'unsaid' against the great meta-narratives of imperial history. It reverses the common notion we have of colonialism as a discourse of domination, subjugation and acquiescence to that of stubborn resistance and confrontation. It also problemmatizes further the difference between official, recorded history and the truth of history. According to Foucault:

> Truth is a thing of this world: it is produced only by virtue of multiple forms of constraints. And it induces regular effects of power. Each society has its regime of truth, its 'general politics of truth': that is, the types of discourse which it accepts and makes function as true; the mechanism and instances which enable one to distinguish true and false statements, the means by which each is sanctioned ; the techniques and procedures accorded value in the acquisition of truth; *the status of those who are charged with saying what counts as true* (1977: 131). (emphasis mine)

Critical studies of the Igbo Women's Revolution of 1929 and 1930, remains an unfinished business. In my thinking, it still poses a lot of questions to scholars of Political Science, Women's Studies and Performance studies world wide. The questions include: How come that the so-called illiterate and uneducated women in a so-called "Third World" were able to stop a colonial law asking them to pay an abominable poll tax in 1929 i.e. at the height of the British imperial powers? What kind of organizational acumen did these women possess. What was the political structure of indigenous, pre-colonial, Igbo society that made it possible for the women to plan, organize and execute this well-orchestrated revolt without a single man knowing about their subterfuge? How did colonialism erode the rights, privileges and political immunities that African women had before the arrival of the British? What did the church and Christian religion contribute to these exercises in cultural vandalism and the political disempowerment of women on the African continent? What was there on the continent as theatre before the arrival of the Europeans and why did theatre and performance play such a pivotal role in the efficacy of this revolution? What insight does this give us when we compare Igbo women's forms of indigenous theatre with what exists in the West today? How does the political status of Igbo women in the 19th and early 20th century, as evident from the historical incident analyzed above, compare with the disenfranchised status of women in England and the USA at the same time in history? Why couldn't women in these democratic and civilized societies vote in their own countries? Since it is true that women in many parts of Igbo land could dethrone a ruler or chief (until recent more "democratic" times) by sitting in on him, what is the significance and relevance of the Igbo women's revolt to the struggle of women all over the world in their bid to gain stronger positions in the political/economic structures and decision-making processes of their societies? Why is it that India, Pakistan, Philipines, and even conservative Britain have produced female political leaders while the USA, the so –

called leader of the free world is yet to produce a female president or vice president? Is it possible that, in the light of what has been discussed above, women in Nigeria in 1929 had more power in the political running of their society and the decision-making processes of their communities, i.e. that they fared better as political free agents than women in England and the USA at this point in history and perhaps even today. How much power, for example, had Emily Wilding Davidson and the Suffragettes at this point in history?

Works Cited

Achebe, Chinua (1984), 'Preface' in *Igbo Arts: Cosmos and Community*, Chike Aniakor and Herbert Cole eds. Los Angeles: Museum of Cultural History

Afigbo, A. E. (1972), *The Warrant Chiefs: Indirect Rule in Southeastern Nigeria 1891-1929* London: Longman.

Allen, Charles (1979), *Tales from the Dark Continent* London: MacDonald & Co Ltd, p.79.

Bakhtin, Mikhail (1965), Rabelais and His World, trans. Helen Iswolski, Bloomington: Indiana University Press

Bhabha, Hommi (1994), *The Location of Culture* London: Routledge.

Bastian, Misty (2002), "'Vultures of the Marketplace': Igbo and Other Southeastern Nigerian Women's Discourse about the *Ogu Umunwaanyi* (Women's War) of 1929" in *Women and African Colonial History*, edited by Jean Allman, Susan Geiger and Nakanyike Musisi eds., Bloomington, IN: Indiana University Press.

Calloway, Helen (1987), *Gender, Culture, Empire: European Women in Colonial Nigeria,*

Fanon, Frantz (1967), *The Wretched of the Earth*. Harmondsworth: Penguin

Foucault, Michel (1977), *Knowledge and Power* New York: Pantheon Books

Mba, Nina (1982), *Nigerian Women Mobilized: Women's Political Activity in Southern Nigeria 1900-1965* Berkeley: Institute of International Studies.

Okpewho, Isidore *et al* (2001), *The African Diaspora* Bloomington: Indiana University Press

Oriji, John (1994), *Traditions of Igbo Origin* New York: Peter Lang.

Public Records Office, London: PRO LO583/176/8. See the Report of Aba Commision of Enquiry, pp.34-60.

Rodney, Walter (19 81), *How Europe Underdeveloped Africa*, Washington DC: Howard University Press

Said, Edward (1994), *Culture and Imperialism*. New York: Vintage Books, 1994).

Schechner Richard (2003), *Performance Studies: An Introduction* New

York: Routledge.

Wangari, Esther (1996), "Feminist Political Ecology" in *Feminist Political Ecology in Global Issues and Local Experiences*. Diane Rocheleau *et al* eds. New York: Routledge, 1996, 287-308.

Young, Robert (1990), *White Mythologies: Writing History and the West*. London: Routledge

Crossing the *Zaure*: Theatre for Development and Women's Empowerment in Northern Nigeria *

Jumai Ewu
University of Northampton, UK

Abstract

Dominant strategies of development in the developing world have been criticised by development activists for failing to involve the participation of people particularly at grassroots level. Until recently, relatively less attention has been paid to how development as a whole has increased the gender gulf, how women continue to be undervalued and suppressed. The focus of this paper is on Theatre for Development (TfD) and women's empowerment in Nigeria.

TfD is a process-driven, grassroots community theatre practice that has emerged to challenge socio-economic and political oppressions that continue to undermine genuine popular participation in development in post-independent Nigeria. Its primary purpose is to utilise popular performance forms to facilitate community participation in development through democratic dialogue, decision-making and collective action. Tar Ahura (1982), one of the pioneers of TfD in Nigeria, had suggested that the task of practitioners is not "to force a cultural revolution on the people but to work within the cultural provisions enhancing credibility and public relations". More than two decades later his views are still echoed by practitioners who are reluctant to rock the boat. The paper examines the evolution of TfD in Nigeria. It highlights the challenges facing the practice in its attempt to facilitate women's participation in development. In the process it evaluates the effectiveness of the strategies employed to date to encourage women's participation in workshops and projects. The paper argues that the factors responsible for the marginalisation of women in development are cultural and economic; that the desire by practitioners not to be perceived as a threat to a community's cultural beliefs and values amounts to a contradiction. It suggests that any genuine attempt to mobilise women through cultural activities must be matched with a commitment to challenge and transform culture itself.

Introduction

The importance of a people centred approach to development is now more or less accepted as given in development discourse. The 1948 United Nations Universal Declaration of Human Rights (UDHR) provided the framework for the debate between the various contending views about development, which gathered momentum in the 1960s and 1970s.This was to culminate in the Declaration on the Right to Development adopted by the United Nations General Assembly in 1986. Development is described as a process of positive socio-economic transformation in the quality and level of human existence aimed at raising the standard of living, quality of life, and human dignity (Freire, 1972; Rodney, 1972, Kidd, and Colletta, (eds.), 1980; Srampickal, 1994). In addition, for development to be meaningful and sustainable, it must involve the participation of people, especially at grassroots level, who form the majority, and must benefit everyone fairly. However, until recently, relatively less attention has been paid to how development as a whole has increased the gender gulf, how women continue to be undervalued and suppressed in all spheres of life. Thus, although there is wide acceptance that the contribution of women to development is high, in real terms their share of the benefits continues to be low. Globally, but even more so in the developing countries, women, like children, remain among the worst victims of poverty. Not only do they have the least access to the means of production, but they receive the least remuneration for their labour also. Furthermore, during periods of socio-economic crisis such as war, civil strife, famine, epidemics, national debt and so on, they along with children, are the main or worst affected victims. Women's poor economic situation is reinforced by their having the least access to the educational system, which would equip them with the knowledge and skills necessary for them to improve their productivity, the least access to political power and to the legal system.

Historically, women have always been perceived as beneficiaries rather than as agents of development. Consequently, development efforts of governments have tended to target men. The beginning of the United Nation's (UN) decade for women (1975-1985) brought increased international attention to the dangers of ignoring half of the world's human resources by focussing development efforts on men only. (Hamrell and Nordberg, eds. 1982). The Convention on the Elimination of all Forms of Discrimination Against Women adopted by the United Nations General Assembly in 1979, sets the minimum benchmark for the elimination of discrimination against women and for the promotion of gender equality. The Convention re-emphasises the call for the integration of women into the entire development process as active participants and equal beneficiaries. This is intended to shift the emphasis away from strategies of welfare and aid that perceive women simply as victims of poverty and oppression to strategies that empower women to actively participate in development by building their capacities and creating equal opportunities and access to means of production and social services. Since its adoption, the Convention has been promoted at world conferences such as the 1993 World Conference on Human Rights held in Vienna, Australia, the 1994 Population and Development Summit in Cairo, Egypt, the 1995 World Summit for Social Development, Copenhagen, Denmark, and the fourth World Conference on Women held in Beijing, China, also in 1995. Complementing such conferences are the more customised initiatives in individual countries undertaken by UN agencies such as the United Nations development Fund for Women (UNIFEM), United Nations Children Fund (UNICEF), United Nations Development Fund (UNDP), United Nations Educational, Scientific and Cultural Organization (UNESCO) and The United Nations Population Fund (UNFPA). Such international interest in the role and well being of women in development has given the issue of gender equality the legitimacy and urgency it lacked before.

In Nigeria, it was within the context of improving the quality of life of women and empowering them to participate in development that government initiatives such as the Better Life for Rural Women Programme (1987), the Family Support Programme (1994), the Family Economic Advancement Programme (1996) and so on were conceived. Well meaning as these and other similar initiatives were, they were flawed in many respects, especially as they failed to sufficiently take into account the role of culture in the process of development. As Ngugi wa Thiong'o points out:

> [i]n many discussions on development, the cultural aspect is left out or else admitted through the back door. And yet if people are the centre of development, if they are both the object and subject of development, then the quality of their cultural life should be the most important indicator of development... what could be a more effective way of making people actors in their own development than to raise awareness and arouse their energies through cultural activities? (1982: 115).

Women constitute a gender and not a social class. Thus, although there are different classes of women with varying access to the means of production, access to power, wealth and general influence, all women in Nigeria are subordinated and discriminated against in terms of gender. Grassroots women, who form the majority of the rural and urban poor, suffer double oppression as a result of both their gender and their social class (Federal Ministry of Women Affairs and United Nations Development Programme, 1996). Women's low social status is a result of, as well as a cause of, their low economic status.

This article is about Theatre for Development (TfD) as a strategy for women's empowerment in Nigeria with particular reference to northern

Nigeria. The aim is to show how, in the attempt to mobilise grassroots participation in development through cultural activities, culture itself is being challenged and transformed. Culture, like human action which it tries to represent and transform, is neither sacrosanct nor static but dynamic

Culture and Development

Nigeria is a multi ethnic, multicultural and multi religious country with a population of over 120 million. The richness of this diversity, and the challenges that it poses for national unity and development are acknowledged in the Nigerian constitution by the provisions made for the rights of Nigerians to develop their culture and to apply it as instrument for promoting national identity and unity. This is also in line with the 1976 UN's International Covenant on Economic, Social and Cultural Rights. However, Nigeria is also inarguably a patriarchal society that is characterised by structural and institutional gender discrimination. It is a society where men dominate the decision making process both in the home and in government.

The Federal Ministry of Culture, Tourism and National Orientation is that arm of government charged with the responsibility of developing and implementing a national policy on culture at federal and states levels. From its title and its activities, the functions of the ministry are primarily economic and Political. The dominant perception of culture is as material culture that can be researched, preserved and marketed. Important as these are, particularly in terms of job creation and the promotion of ethnic identities and national unity, the idea of culture as ideology and its interface with development almost becomes an after thought except in an overtly political sense. Without a doubt patriarchal hegemony and the gender inequality that it fosters pose a serious obstacle to sustainable development.

Gender is culturally constructed because social roles and standards of behaviour are determined by cultural norms and values rather than by what women can do for themselves. Ngugi wa Thiong'o (1981) explains that it is the group or groups with the political power who control all the machinery of state power who also control the values and world outlook of the rest of society. Gramsci's theory of hegemony describes the process of gaining the consent of subordinate groups, a process whereby dominant groups maintain their power and control over cultural institutions and activities by making these appear as common sense or the norm (Williams, 1977: 108-114). Patriarchal hegemony is entrenched in the social structure and is perpetuated by beliefs, customs, norms and values that have their roots in indigenous Nigerian cultural systems, in Islam, Christianity, and colonialism. Essentially, it is through the process of socialisation in a specific culture that the cultural expectations of male / female roles and behaviour are inculcated.

Althusser (1984: 1-60) recognises that cultural institutions such as the family, the law, politics, the arts, religion, the education system and the mass media are the vehicle of ideology and therefore the institutions through which hegemony is exercised, reinforced and reproduced. At the same time they become sites for conflict as the various groups struggle for means and occasions to express themselves there.

Because gender is culturally constructed, attitudes and behaviours can be changed. The same cultural institutions can be usefully appropriated to mobilise and to energise every member of the society to contribute fully to development.

Theatre as Cultural Intervention

The current status of the performing arts in Nigeria, compared to that of other forms of cultural production would seem to indicate that they have very little to contribute to national development beyond their economic value. There appears to be very little investment by government in the performing arts beyond infrastructures such as the occasional theatre building and hosting of large cultural festivals. Whereas the mass media such as radio, television, film, and the home video industry receive some measure of recognition, the performing arts, particularly theatre, receive little such acknowledgement except in times of acute national crisis when they are appropriated to consciously influence people's behaviour Politically. For example, the significance of educational television broadcast to schools was acknowledged in 1959, the same year that television broadcasting began in Nigeria. In addition, today, each of the thirty-six states of the federation as well as the federal territory in Abuja has a Nigerian Television Authority (NTA) station while some states have an additional state owned television station. All of these are largely under state control and are funded by the state. The development of the performing arts, on the other hand, is largely left to local communities, the universities and individual artists. While few would argue for or support any form of government control of the performing arts, various disguises of state censorship already take place without an equivalent financial support.

Theatre is a cultural institution and is at the same time a form of cultural production. As such it is a vehicle of ideology. This notion is imaginatively captured in Richard Schechner's and Victor Turner's 'infinity loop', and in their interrogation of the relationship between social and aesthetic drama (Schechner, 1988: 187-193). Unlike literature, theatre not only seeks to reflect social reality but to affect it as well. Its relationship with social reality can be reactive as well as proactive, setting the agenda, exploring and showing what is, as well as what is possible. In the process, it can itself be transformed. Soyinka puts it this way:

We must not forget that drama, like any other art form, is created and executed within a specific physical environment. It naturally interacts with that environment, is influenced by it, influences that environment in turn and acts together with the environment in the larger and far more complex history of society... (1993: 134).

Theatre is situated in the here and now, lending it a sense of immediacy and of the contemporary. As dramatic action, theatre depicts what people choose to do or not to do when confronted by certain circumstances, and the consequences of their decisions. It is a dynamic medium that shows dynamic characters in dynamic situations where anything is possible. But theatre is also much more than these. Nigerian theatre, for example, is multi disciplinary and multi functional. Studies of extant and contemporary forms and practices reveal a variety of traditions existing simultaneously. Despite their differences, the tendency of Nigerian theatre is to reproduce, maintain and reinforce the dominant patriarchal structures of power though there are occasions when they can be used to challenge and to subvert the status quo. The role of theatre in pre and post independent socio-political and economic struggles in Nigeria is exemplified by the works of artists of the literary and popular travelling genres such as Hurbert Ogunde, Wole Soyinka, Ola Rotimi, J.P. Clark-Bekederemo, Bode Sowande, Femi Osofisan, among many others. In the minority are female playwrights such as Zulu Sofola, Tess Onwueme, and Stella Moroundia Oyedebo, championing the cause for gender equality and women's empowerment with varying degrees of success. Despite the attempt to combine western dramaturgical techniques and styles with more localised and indigenous Nigerian performance forms, the appeal and impact of Nigerian literary drama has been limited, especially at grassroots level. Its audiences have continued to be largely drawn from among the western educated and school going population.

Potentially much more effective in addressing the issue of the role and participation of women in sustainable social change is TfD, a process driven, grassroots community theatre practice that is a part of a growing global movement that began about the middle part of the twentieth century particularly in the developing continents of Latin America, Asia and Africa. TfD intends to challenge dominant trends of cultural representations, presentations and social relations and to facilitate sustainable development in communities at grassroots level. It is designed to use popular performance forms to facilitate the active participation of rural and urban grassroots communities in collectively researching, identifying, analysing and communicating development issues with a view to solving them (Abah, 2003). As such the social relationships articulated in the process of creation, presentation, and reception, become just as crucial to it as those articulated in the specific and more contained theatrical performances that form part of its process. These subtle aspects form part of the meanings generated and communicated through the practice. In other words, the question of who performs or is allowed to perform is just as crucial to it as what is performed, how, where, when, and why. In principle, there are no spectators in TfD. All are actively involved in a process of mutual learning, empowerment and action. As a process of theatre creation emerging from the community, it is culture in the making, constantly challenging and transforming in many complex ways, and in turn is being challenged and transformed as participants' understanding of their situation deepens and they explore the possibilities of action and the implications of each course of action (Srampickal,1994).

However, TfD's practice has come under increasing scrutiny amidst criticism from within as from without for wittingly or unwittingly viewing its constituencies in monolithic terms. Until recently, its practice and discourse has at best been gender neutral and shrouded in such terms as 'the people', 'the oppressed', 'the grassroots communities, the 'marginalised' and so on. At worst, TfD has generally addressed itself to men despite the fact that the female population is higher than the male's in its primary constituencies, the rural and urban working class areas. In many practices it is assumed that community participation means men speaking for and acting on behalf of every other social group. For a practice that prides itself in demystifying cultural structures and processes, TfD has seemed powerless, at times even reluctant, to turn its attention to those that are rooted in patriarchy. As Paulo Freire, one of its influences, puts it:

> To be oppressed is to be emotionally, psychologically and economically dependent on another. An act is oppressive when it prevents another from being fully human...any situation in which 'A' objectively exploits 'B' or hinders his [sic] pursuit of self affirmation as a responsible person is an act of oppression. Such a situation in itself constitutes violence, even when sweetened by false generosity...(Freire, 1972: 31).

The marginalisation of women in TfD is reflective of their marginalisation in society in general. It is perpetuated by the dominant patriarchal structures from within which the practice operates and by weaknesses in its methodology.

TfD in Northern Nigeria

TfD in Nigeria emerged in the mid 1970s in the activities of the then drama section of the English Department of Ahmadu Bello University (ABU) Zaria, the oldest federal university in northern Nigeria, particularly in its Samaru and Community theatre projects (Amkpa, 2004: 95). For more than two decades after that ABU remained primarily the singular seat of the practice in Nigeria. However, since the 1990s, the practice has not only spread beyond the confines of undergraduate and graduate drama programmes and into the surrounding communities but even further to other parts of the country. Today, there exist a number of practices that are distinguishable in terms of their contexts: academically based practices located in the curriculum of Colleges and Universities departments of drama or theatre arts, practices located in the activities of Non Governmental Organisations, and those that form part of the output of independent professional theatre companies.

To a large extent, there is a general agreement among the different practices in terms of philosophy, aims, and methodologies. However, essentially, TfD is a context specific practice. The detail and emphasis of each practice is determined by factors such as the geographical location of its activities, the local economies, and the dominant cultures of the area including language, religion and performance traditions. Thus as far as gender expectations and the impact that they have on the practice are concerned, these may vary, even if only slightly, from one geographic community to another, or even from time to time within the same community such as between the Muslim north and the non-Muslim middle and southern parts of the country; between the more cosmopolitan urban communities and the rural communities. There is a sense in which the history of TfD in Nigeria as a whole is tied to the history of its evolution in Zaria. Therefore, this discussion will focus largely on the activities of Zaria which still remains the epicentre of the practice in the north. However, wherever it is necessary, references will be made to other areas as well.

The city of Zaria is located in the northern part of Nigeria, specifically in Kaduna state (present day Nigeria is divided into thirty six states). Although the city is predominantly Hausa speaking, Islamic, and culturally conservative, it consists of various settlements such as Sabon Gari, Zaria City, Tudun Wada, Wusasa, Gyelesu, Samaru, Palladan, and so on, each with its own distinct characteristics. The Hausa is the dominant ethnic group in northern Nigeria and is patrilineal, predominantly Muslim and polygamous. In the Muslim areas, *purdah*, a system which confines women to the domestic space and prevents their active participation in public life is widely practiced particularly in the rural areas. The *Zaure* is the Hausa word for the large entrance porch that leads into the main traditional residential compound and often doubles as a male reception area. You cross the *Zaure* to reach the walled compound where the women's living quarters are located. Therefore, the *Zaure* may be considered as a symbol of, or metaphor for male supremacy. It is an appropriate symbol for a patriarchal society where men rule the roost at home and outside it, and are society's gatekeepers and opinion leaders. That a practice so radical in its intentions should emerge from this city may seem ironic at first. However, sometimes the most challenging situations can be the most stimulating and provide the impetus for creativity and innovation. Besides, the location of the drama section within a highly politicised Faculty of Arts and Social Sciences partly contributed to its growth. Equally of note is the fact that Zaria, despite its cultural conservatism, was the seat of power of the legendary 16th century Queen Amina of Zazzau, the formidable warrior who fought and conquered many of the kingdoms that constitute contemporary northern Nigeria.

Academic Based Practices: The Samaru and Community Theatre Projects

Drama was established as a degree programme at ABU in 1975 under the leadership of Michael Etherton, renowned TfD practitioner and development activist. From the start the Samaru and Community Theatre projects were part of the undergraduate and graduate curriculum.

With their emphases on practice, three groups of participants can be identified working collaboratively on the two projects: the teaching staff, whom we may want to call trainer-practitioners, the students and the communities. However, the two projects differ from each other in the details of their objectives, their mode of operation and in the communities involved.

The Samaru project is an annual community outreach programme involving second year (formerly first year of a three year programme) undergraduate drama students devising performances on issues derived from research conducted in the satellite community of Samaru. The community, which is separated from the university's main campus by the Zaria – Sokoto highway is multi ethnic, multi religious and predominantly working class. A large proportion of the population is literate or semi literate. Women form part of the labour market with many engaged in one form of income generation activity or the other as employees of the university, the local banks, primary schools, local government, or as self employed petty traders in the local market or within the vicinity of the home. While the dominant culture exercises its hegemony, the community is less conservative than the more homogenous, Hausa speaking villages located a little further away from the university.

In the drama department, the number of male students tends to be higher than female students and this continues right up to the level of the trainer-practitioners. The history of education in Nigeria as a whole, and in northern Nigeria in particular, is one of unequal opportunities for women compared to men. Pre-colonial customs and values, religious ideologies, and colonial educational policies and practices have, in the past, all united in their mission to keep women subordinated. While current policies within the education sector to empower women are beginning to have an effect on the statistics, gender imbalance, especially at tertiary level, continues to be noticeable. In fields of study such as drama or theatre arts, the number of registered female students is on the increase. However, the majority of these are drawn from the non-Muslim areas of the North and the Middle Belt because Islam frowns upon any form of artistic representation of humans, more so where these forms are perceived to have their roots in 'pagan' practices. In addition, the values of extreme female modesty and chastity inhibit any form of public displays or self-promotion by women.

In terms of its process, the Samaru Project involves students spending about one week gathering information through face-to-face interviews in order to identify issues and problems significant to the Samaru residents. From the start students are encouraged to be aware of the mediating ideologies of their privileged class position in relation to the members of the community however, less stress is placed on gender as a defining aspect of identity. They engage residents in discussions and observe modes of behaviour, expressions, cultural practices and values. At the end of this exercise, the students return to the university based studio theatre where, in a whole group plenary session, they compare and share their experiences with one another. Through guided discussion and analysis students try to arrive at a deeper understanding of the information gathered. Such understanding is then used to rank the issues in order of priority and to decide which of these would be explored further in the process of play making.

The next stage involves students working in two or three sub groups to devise open air dramatic pieces on the issues which they return to perform in strategically identified locations on the streets of Samaru. Performances are usually in Hausa or Pidgin English, itself widely spoken, with translator – narrators for each.

Where performances end at the point of crisis or with questions, they are open ended and flexible, allowing room for discussion during and post the performance. Improvisation, storytelling, mime, dramatic enactment, song and dance are some of the forms drawn upon. The early evening is the preferred time and the audience consists largely of male adults, children and relatively fewer women.

On its own part, the annual community theatre project involves third year (formerly second year of a three year programme) drama students working with one or more rural communities located further away from the university such as the villages of Bomo, Hayin Dogo, Tudun Sarki and Palladan. These are relatively more culturally homogenous and conservative than Samaru, predominantly Hausa speaking, Muslim, and agrarian. Here, the *purdah* system is in force. Young girls of school age engage in hawking outside the home as a way of helping their mothers earn some modest income.

While following the same process as Samaru, the Community Theatre Project is very different in one crucial area. Despite the conservatism of the communities involved, there is a greater community involvement throughout the process. This is largely due to an improved methodology that enables the presence and participation of volunteer members of the community, many of whom are drawn from Community Based Organisations. (CBOs). Meetings, discussions and performances all take place in the communities. And, where the communities are located quite far away from the University, the students lodge in the villages for the duration of the project. Such increased contact and exchange with the community establishes a different kind of relationship between the project and the community. Usually the plays that emerge from the process are much more organic to the communities, and attract larger numbers of villagers who turn out to watch their friends, relatives, and neighbours perform stories about the problems and issues concerning their communities, and to participate in the debates.

Graduate students participate in both projects as trainer-practitioners. Over the years, the general template of the Samaru and Community Theatre processes have been adapted as the practice continues to evolve and spread to other parts of the country. Today, they serve as models for undergraduate and graduate community theatre programmes at other universities departments of drama, theatre, or performing arts such as Katsina Ala, Jos, Abuja, Maiduguri, Ibadan, Benin and Lagos. Practitioners are in agreement that of the two, the Community Theatre Project provides a better model for developing an effective and sustainable TfD practice in Nigeria. As a model, it has been adapted, with varying degrees of success, by NGOs and Independent Theatre Company practices. The unique and positive experience of living in the community throughout the duration of the project has now been formalised into what is known as the *Homestead* approach or method. However, despite these achievements, a major problem that the two projects (and their adapted forms in other parts of the country) have shared over the years is their inability to engage women as actively as the men throughout their processes. The more culturally conservative the community is, the more challenging it becomes for the projects to involve women. In the case of Samaru and other non-Muslim communities in, for example, the Middle Belt and southern parts of the country, there are other factors besides *purdah* which prove equally effective in preventing their active involvement. Socio-economic factors, which are nonetheless rooted in patriarchy, such as the double work load outside and within the home, and their attendant issues are proving to be effective barriers.

In 1982, concerned about the lack of women's participation in its projects the drama department sought the support and mediation of a prominent female politician from Zaria City, Hajiya Gambo Sawaba. The proposed project was to be modelled on the Samaru project and would involve an all female group of students. The devised theatre pieces would be toured round purdah households to predominantly female audiences in Samaru, Sabon Gari and Zaria City. Both Sabon Gari and Zaria City, large settlements of the city of Zaria are located in close proximity in the centre of the city. Sabon Gari is large, sprawling, and the commercial heartland of the city. As can be expected, it attracts settlers from all parts of the country. However, despite its multi ethnic, multi religious composition, the dominant Hausa, Islamic culture maintains its hegemonic influence. In contrast, Zaria City, the original site of Zaria before its expansion, is much more culturally homogenous. It is the seat of the emirate and still boasts the ancient wall that defines its boundaries and protects its cultural identity. That the project was able to scale its wall and cross the Zaure to reach the women was in itself a decisive achievement in the history of the evolution of TfD practice in Zaria. The two devised pieces, *Dillaliya* and *Duniya Juyi Juyi*, were based on issues identified by the women in the communities as important to them namely, the break down of marriages and the value of female education. However, due to entrenched gender bias and the fact that it required the consent of the male heads of households, the project was limited in what it could achieve. Censorship, and even self-censorship, governed the decision making process and the choices that could be made. Practically, it was impossible to achieve more than a few visits or to engage the women in any lengthy discussions. Likewise, the research period was short, and limited to information gathering without much exploration of women's popular performance forms. Devised by young female students, the emphasis was on tightly structured, close ended, finished performances rather than on the process itself. In the end, the status quo was left intact, though as an experiment, the project managed to highlight what was possible.

Non-Governmental Organizations

For decades both projects, especially the Samaru Project, have tackled the same issues year in year out with very little impact. Instead of decreasing, their repertoire of issues continues to increase. Perhaps not surprisingly, the number of students, especially female students who, upon graduation, pursue careers in TfD, or in Community Theatre in general continues to be small. 'Nothing succeeds like success' is a famous educational tenet. The involvement of CBOs in the Community Theatre Project has yielded a small crop of TfD devotees. The association of these individuals with the drama department has been mutually beneficial. While these individuals have been instrumental in widening the participation of communities through their organisations, the department has provided training in TfD skills. It was in order to increase community participation that the drama department, and its associate CBOs came together to form the Zaria Popular Theatre Alliance (ZAPTA) in 1986. ZAPTA became one way of establishing an organisational base outside the university and extending TfD practice beyond the confines of the undergraduate and graduate programmes. It was considered to be a more effective organ for facilitating skills transfer to communities and increasing the possibility of follow-up action by them. At the same time, the success from the grassroots level would provide greater incentive for students to specialise in this area of theatre practice. Amidst all these developments, the low participation of women continued to be a vexed issue. The CBOs initially involved, Haske (Samaru), So Dangi (Hayin Dogo), and Muna Fata (Palladan), happened to be all male social clubs. One exception to the membership of ZAPTA was Women in Nigeria (WIN), a national women's organisation. However, at the time, there were other organisations besides those in ZAPTA that existed in Samaru and other parts of the city. It is widely known that there are many ethnic cultural organisations to be found in every urban town or city in Nigeria, many of which have their women's wing. These grassroots cultural organisations are formed in order to support and promote the socio-economic development of their members whilst celebrating their cultural identity through periodic cultural activities. These were resources that were yet to be tapped into at the time.

While ZAPTA provided the model and foundation for the formation of The Nigerian Popular Theatre Alliance (NPTA) (Amkpa, 2004: 97), it is the latter, particularly through its zonal and national training workshops and conferences, that has been most influential in the expansion of TfD practice not only to the curriculum of other university departments of drama and theatre arts but throughout the country as well. NPTA is a nation wide none governmental voluntary organisation inaugurated in Zaria in 1989 under the leadership of Oga Abah (Ewu, 1999: 98). Its function is to bring together professional and voluntary theatre practitioners, educationists, and cultural and development workers interested in using theatre for development purposes. A key objective of the organisation is to encourage and to support the practices of its members, and to facilitate the expansion of TfD practice nationwide. The activities of NPTA generally include convening international, national, and zonal TfD workshops and conferences while member groups and individuals run outreach and training workshops and projects locally and further beyond as determined by their experience and reputation. Most of these workshops, some of which target issues affecting women, have been funded by partner international voluntary and governmental agencies such as the Mass Mobilisation for Self Reliance, Social Justice and Economic Recovery (MAMSER), Canadian University Services Overseas (CUSO), the McArthur Foundation, and UNICEF.

The work of NPTA at its headquarters in Zaria has been complemented by the Renaissance Theatre Network (RTN), a TfD organisation led by Steve Daniel with its base in ABU. RTN is said to work in close collaboration with 'a web of community based theatre groups that have their own internal dynamics and focus on a wide range of significant community action…' (International Human Rights Law Group, 2003: 17). In addition to its own projects, RTN offers training in dramatic skills to CBOs and drama groups. These include such CBOs as 'Bayajidda Social and Dramatic Club, Funtua, Munji Mun Gani from Giwa, Tawakaltu Social and Dramatic Club, Sabon Gari, Gamji Social and Dramatic Club, Sodangi Social Club, Hayin Dogo, and Inganci'(30). The combined effects of the curriculum based courses, NPTA and RTN on TfD practice in Zaria has been significant. NPTA's research and documentation centre located on the main campus of the university ensures that TfD itself continues to develop in response to wider social changes. Collectively, the practices have enabled a slight, but inarguably, visible increase in women's participation in TfD. Their collaborations with CBOs, some of which, following the examples of their mentors, now include women in their membership, are beginning to make a difference. For example, Bayajidda Social and Dramatic Club now includes female members. Located in Funtua, Katsina State, an area under the jurisdiction of the Islamic *Sharia* law, makes this a remarkable achievement. The women, many of whom are former prostitutes, arguably represent some of the most exploited and marginalised groups in the society. The community theatre projects involving these CBOs have inspired a more positive image of their female members. From being viewed as a breeding ground for prostitutes, the public's perception of theatre is beginning to shift to it being an instrument for the reclamation and rehabilitation of broken lives. Additional support from women's organisations and other progressive NGOs which sometimes partner NPTA and RTN on projects is also contributing to this slow but certain transformation. The theme of collaboration, which runs through these projects, collaboration between men and women, between academic institution and CBOs, and between CBOs and Local Government organs and agencies, has been decisive in achieving the sustainability of both TfD practice and development at grassroots level. Even more will be achieved when membership of women in these organisations spreads, or better still, when more grassroots women's organisations are involved.

WIN has been a member of NPTA from the start and to date remains the only member to wholly and consistently address gender issues. Established in 1982 with Ayesha Imam as its president, its initial base was in the sociology department of the Faculty of Arts and Social Sciences. Currently, WIN is one of the most established and politicised women's organisations in Nigeria with its headquarters in Lagos. It is an organisation aimed specifically at women but with membership open to men as well. According to its mission statement, WIN is set up to 'make policy on, and take action aimed at improving the conditions of women' (WIN, 1982a). Its intention was to use such activities as research, conferences, public representation, and meetings to provide:

> the means through which effective strategies and campaigns might be developed and fought in the continuing struggle against women's oppression (WIN, 1982b).

Initially, the overall membership of WIN was middle class. In this it followed a pattern that has been repeated in most developing countries, where literate urban women, who are often more economically independent, and therefore wield more political power, lead the struggle for women's emancipation. The question of whether or not the aims and activities of such organisations are compromised by their middle class identities is an on going debate. Suffice to say that WIN is an organisation that believes in self-advocacy as a strategy for women's empowerment, and recognises the need for progressive alliances with similar minded organisations such as the Nigerian Labour Congress, grassroots co-operatives, Academic Staff Union of Universities and Student Unions. The concern to reach out to, and be relevant to grassroots women is one that WIN shares with the drama department and with NPTA in general. This was what led to the forging of a partnership between it and the department from the start. The idea, then, was that TfD would become a vital tool for WIN's operations. Reciprocally, WIN would provide the practice with the organisational base, structural support, information, and funding that it needed to facilitate the continuity of its projects.

The first of their collaborations was facilitated by Salihu Bappa, a trainer-practitioner, and an associate member of WIN. This took place in 1984 in the form of a pilot project that targeted the university community. The play that was devised tackled the topical issue of the increasing frequency of rape on the university's main campus. Increasing pressures to address cultural issues that affect women's health such as unequal distribution of labour, infant mortality, early marriage, teenage pregnancy, and Female Genital Mutilation (FGM) led to another collaborative project in 1984. The project addressed medical and social complications that develop when young girls, sometimes as early as twelve years old are married off for cultural reasons.

The drama that emerged, titled *The Dilemma of Womanhood* was a product of a collaborative process between the department, WIN, community nurses and other health workers from Yakawada Comprehensive Health Centre (Abah, O. *et al.* n.d.). It was performed by nurses and health workers, and to a mixed audience of midwives, patients, and community heads from the surrounding communities. The plot proposed female education as a solution to the problem and shared the responsibility for change equally between community leaders, policy makers, and parents on the one hand, and women themselves on the other.

Post performance discussions attempted to take on board factors that helped or hindered treatment and rehabilitation and, quite significantly, patriarchal ideologies that engendered the problem. Equally significant was the fact that the majority of the performers were female health workers who had first hand information about the problem from their patients whose lives they tried to represent. However, as the audience of the drama, the patients' own experience was on the whole, little more than as voyeurs. It would have required the patients themselves to perform in order to deal with the more complicated issues of agency involved. The experience of crossing the spatial boundary and physically performing would have been one further step towards challenging those cultural factors that engendered the problem in the first place (Boal, 1979). However, the collaboration showed a much more improved practice than hitherto. Some few years later, in 1989, the Theatre for Integrated Development (TIDE) workshops held by NPTA in the three rural communities of Otobi, Adankari, and Onyuwei of Benue State was to demonstrate just what collaborations with grassroots women's organisations can achieve in performance terms (Illah, 2005; Harding, 1999).

Singularly and in their collaborations, NPTA and WIN have grown since those early days. The general political climate in Nigeria as a whole today means that gender, as an issue can no longer be ignored. The aftermath of the Beijing conference in 1995, and the increasing contact with other parts of the world through international travel, and developments in technology such as satellite television and the Internet have generated a myriad of women's organisations across the country. In terms of their composition, some of these are local and others are national; some are religious based and others are secular, some are cultural while others are business and professional. Each of the organisations has a mission statement which identifies the specific issues with which it is concerned such as education, law, health, the media, human rights, children and youth, the environment, and so on. In real terms, there are thousands of women's co-operatives, associations and organisations located in rural and urban areas across the country. Although many of these describe their activities as none political, there are now more politicised women's organisations than when WIN first started out. Such organisations are taking the issue of women's rights on, particularly in the areas of politics and citizenship, education, health, the law, the mass media, and the environment. Significantly, many of them would like to incorporate theatre in their activities but are hindered by lack of skills and funds. Here exists a strong potential for collaboration with training institutions such as universities departments of drama and theatre for mutual benefits. Women's empowerment and role in development will be greatly enhanced by their participation in such cultural activities as TfD and vice versa.

Independent Theatre Companies

Contemporary professional theatre companies, with the exception of the popular travelling theatre variety of the likes of Ogunde, Baba Sala and Jagua, are of a much rare breed in Nigeria. Operated as businesses, and run by graduates of drama and theatre arts, they are located in urban towns and cities, and are comparable to the University arts theatres. Generally under funded, they constantly battle to survive. Many have found that the more diversified their activities, and their audiences, the more chances they have to survive. In part strategic and in part responding to the general mood in the country, many are beginning to incorporate TfD objectives and approaches to their creative processes and outputs but are still limited by time and funds. Voluntary and semi professional drama groups or associations, whose members have other full time jobs, often describe themselves as NGOs. There are increasing numbers of these operating at grassroots levels. Partnership between these and university departments of drama and theatre arts, and with organisations such as NPTA and RTN, is enabling their acquisition of TfD skills that are useful and more effective for their operations at grassroots level.

All TfD practices in their different contexts have potential for promoting gender equality and empowering women to participate actively in development. Together, they provide a rich variety of means of using theatre to mediate and to facilitate socio-economic change.

Problems of Methodologies

The factors hindering the effectiveness of TfD in enabling women's participation at grassroots level are not only cultural but methodological as well. TfD's philosophy and principles are sufficiently inclusive and robust to embrace all senses of the oppressed and marginalised including women and children. Rather, it is in the interpretation and translation of these into practice that it continues to fail women. Self-censorship and the tendency to make one template fit all play a big part in this. The tendency to not want to 'rock the boat' often limits its revolutionary potential and cripples creativity and innovation. Furthermore, it is insufficient for men, whether as cultural or as development activists, as husbands, bosses, practitioners, policy makers, theoreticians, analysts, and so on to speak for women no matter how well intentioned. Similarly, it is insufficient to have a situation where invariably urban elite women represent rural women because the former's class privileges remain intact. TfD has the capacity to change these through the extension of its training programmes to grassroots communities and in its collaborations with women's organisations. But it may entail a more specific and fitter for purpose approach that what currently obtains.

Research, analysis, devising, performance, discussions and implementation of action plans, are crucial aspects of a TfD process, and what define its methodology across practices though not necessarily restricted to this order. Close scrutiny of the workings of any of these aspects reveal the need for them to be adapted to suit the unique situation of women. For example, the preliminary research phase, which tends to occur at the early stages of a TfD process, involves identifying and gathering information on community issues. That this research is not simply in order to create 'truthful' performances but also to understand the people, establish trust, and to find the most appropriate ways to contextualise, problematise, analyse and collectively find solutions to the problems has been made clear (Abah, 2003). The *Homestead* and *Community Mapping* are the most favoured approaches to information gathering. Employed within these are the techniques of observation, face-to-face interview, group discussion, and cultural batter in which knowledge and skills of performance forms are exchanged between participants. Culturally, men predominate in household and community decision-making. Thus the success rate of an interview, particularly with women in *purdah*, depends to a large extent on the cooperation of husbands or household heads. The absence or objection of husbands or heads of households can easily prevent the participation of women. Even in none *purdah* communities, community heads and opinion leaders tend to be men and hegemonic values of modesty further contribute to silencing women or tempering what they can say about themselves publicly, and to whom. While the fewer number of women engaged in the practice continues to constitute a problem there is also, the ambivalent attitude of grassroots women themselves to female facilitators. There are as many reports of women finding it easier to engage in dialogue with women exclusive of men as there are of them to better believe men, and to place more weight on their words. What these indicate is that even the research techniques employed must be scrutinised and where necessary, more appropriate methods and techniques that can cross these invisible barriers will need to be explored and used.

The stage following the preliminary research is often described as an analysis stage. However, it is generally acknowledged that analysis is endemic to the TfD process and goes on all the time as participants engage in discussions and decision-making. Analysis is a useful activity engaged in by all participants in order to come to a shared understanding of the issues involved. It is what is at the heart of any conscientisation process, a process that may be described as qualitative education. Where gender, as a mediating factor, is ignored or suppressed then an incomplete or false understanding is reached. With its stress on class differentiation orthodox Marxist analysis, which still largely informs the practice, often ignores the influence of culture on women's participation in development. This is compounded by the desire by practitioners not to be perceived as a threat to a community's cultural beliefs and values; not to make people feel uncomfortable.

Reporting on a 1982 Benue International Popular Theatre Workshop that took place in Nigeria, the late Tar Ahura, one of the key facilitators said of one stage of the workshop process in Igyura village:

> There was a lengthy group discussion in the reception hall of the village head from which women were excluded. Women in this society are only

seen in public and not heard except with their husband's permission. Even so, they must speak the minds of their husbands. Since popular theatre is a cultural action efforts must be made to respect the ways of the people as a way of establishing credibility (Ahura, 1982: 60).

He went on to explain that as far as they, as cultural activists, could understand:

their assignment was not to force a cultural revolution on the people but to work within the cultural provisions enhancing credibility and public relations (61).

The prevalence of this view is confirmed by reports on more recent projects (Mike, & Members of PSW, 1999: 61-78; Amkpa, 2004: 98-104). Clearly, there is a need to strike a delicate balance between demonstrating respect and sensitivity to people's cultures on the one hand, and promoting and protecting the rights of women on the other. The intention of TfD is to draw upon the cultural strengths of the people. The technique of cultural batter is one that offers a great deal of potential for integrating human / women's rights into the entire process but is currently under utilised in favour of more verbal techniques

The development and performance making stage continues the process of analysis with the added task of encoding the issues in a performative form that will communicate to participants on various levels. The aim is to develop performances that will stimulate critical consciousness and empower every member of the community to actively participate in effecting positive socio-economic change. Where the research done in the early stages has been thorough enough to include researching into the most effective and inclusive forms, and where the analysis is extended to include a critical interrogation of these, the tendency to fall back on forms which may seem easy and pragmatic at the time but contradictory in terms of the purpose of the practice, especially where women are concerned, may be minimised. Conventional Western dramatic form is well known for its history of gender bias. Indigenous pre-colonial performance forms demonstrate similar gender bias with genres divided along gender lines. Some performance forms are more associated with one gender than the other. Among these are oral traditions and performances associated with various rites of passage, occupational forms, and ceremonial community festivals. However, there are some genres that are common to both males and females, although the context in which they are performed may differ. Storytelling, praise singing, and dance are typical examples. It is possible for TfD to tap into all these genres, including the most ritualistic and patriarchal of them, and also to revision them.

Indigenous Nigerian performance forms are adaptable and continue to adapt in response to wider social changes in society. Their survival and continued relevance depends on this quality. Soyinka explains:

> when we consider art forms from the point of view of survival strategies, the dynamics of cultural interaction with society become even more aesthetically challenging and fulfilling. We discover, for instance, that under certain conditions some art forms are transformed into others – simply to ensure the survival of the threatened forms. Drama may give way to poetry and song in order to disseminate dangerous sentiments under the watchful eye of the oppressor, the latter forms being more easily communicable. On the other hand, drama may become more manifestly invigorated in order to counteract the effect of an alienating environment (1993: 134-135).

The Kwagh-hir puppet theatre of the Tiv of Benue State, and the more general art of storytelling are some good examples.

The Samaru Project experimented with one such form in the mid-1980s. Sauna and Dauda were two male 'stock characters' who featured across a number of projects as a way of providing the audiences with characters they could grow to recognise and identify with (Amkpa, 2004: 99). Sauna was derived from a Hausa popular comic cartoon strip character and transplanted to the community outreach project to facilitate easy communication as well as to provide some organic thread through the various issues and experiences that the projects dealt with. The original cartoon features the farcical escapades of its protagonist, Sauna. Comparable to animal trickster characters popular in many folk tales, Sauna constantly over reaches himself. Like the tales, the female characters that appear in *Sauna* only play supporting roles. Both genres present many opportunities for gender revisioning but this did not happen on the project. As a result the women that featured in the performances were assigned their traditional passive / victim roles while the issues were perceived and addressed from the dominant male perspective of Dauda and Sauna. Both functioned as narrator-facilitators, mediating between the stories enacted and the 'realities' of the audiences' lives. They had the freedom to engage in dialogue with persons on either side of the narrative frame as they flitted in and out of the world of the story and that of the audience. The use of male narrators failed to acknowledge the role of women in storytelling, and to empower women to be protagonists of the action.

TfD performances are intended to continue the process of analysis by engaging all participants in dialogue. The extent to which they are effective in achieving this is determined by the effectiveness of the previous stages. Described as the most concentrated part of most community theatre processes (Kershaw, 1992), the dramatic performance commands a lot of attention as various project reports show. Such concentration may prove more restrictive than other more loose and inclusive forms such as festival drama. The festival has a lot to offer a practice such as TFD in terms of its context, its loose structure, and the variety of performance forms that it can accommodate, the abundance of opportunities for impersonation, subversion, and role reversal, and its ability to appeal to both the emotions as well as the intellect. With festivals, the meanings articulated extend beyond what can or is verbalised. Again as Soyinka points out:

> The level of organisation involved, the integration of the sublime with the mundane, the endowment of the familiar with properties of the unique (and this spread over days) all indicate that it is into the heart of many African festivals that we should look for the most stirring expressions of man's [sic] instincts and need for drama at its most comprehensive and community involving (1993: 138).

The *Kallankuwa* (meaning a show for everyone) annual festival of Bomo village is a famous example of one such Hausa festival that has evolved from its ritualistic roots as a community harvest festival where everyone is a participant as a spectator and as a performer (Etherton, 1982; International Human Rights Law Group, 2003). It is where everyone goes to see and to be seen. The festival has had close association with the drama department since the latter's establishment. The 2003 festival was a close collaboration between CBOs and drama groups, the International Human Rights Law Group, and RTN under the general theme of 'Voter Education and Mobilisation' in the run up to the 2003 General Elections (International Human Rights Law Group, 2003). That year, the format of the festival was replicated in different towns and villages in Kaduna and in the neighbouring states of Katsina and Kano in what was described as 'the ripple effect' It invited participation from NGOs from around the country including women's organisations such as the League for Democratic Women (LEADS), the Legislative Coalition on Violence Against Women (LACVAW), the Raising Hope for Women and Child, as well as from the Federal Ministry of Women's Affairs. Their involvement was aimed at raising awareness on the significance of women's active participation in Politics and related issues. In general, the participation of grassroots women in the festival itself, including the dramatic performances, was still relatively marginal but significant (International Human Rights Law Group, 2003).

For festival drama, the space of performance in concrete spatial terms and in terms of the opportunity it provides to play with notions of the real and the imagined often generates sufficient license for normal rules of social roles between male and female to be challenged. Thus the potential for TfD to challenge patriarchy lies not just in the unconventional structure of its process but can extend into even highly concentrated moments of performaces. Whatever forms are employed will need to be interrogated for the opportunities they afford women to represent themselves or to subvert the status quo. Ultimately, what all the stages of the process should be leading towards is the empowerment of grassroots communities to participate in development. Where the process works to engage women actively, the chances of translating this into real action are enhanced. This may require the emergence of TfD groups whose main agenda would be to address development issues from the perspective of women, working in collaboration with other women's organisations. The shift from advocacy by well-intentioned practitioners to self-advocacy can only be achieved when grassroots women take centre stage and speak for themselves. Only then can genuine participation be said to take place.

References

Abah, O. S. et al (n.d.), *Silence and Bridges: Report of the Nigerian Popular Theatre Alliance (NPTA) – Women in Nigeria (WIN) Workshops* on ' Women's Health', Unpublished.

Abah, O. S. (ed.) (2003) *Geographies of Citizenship in Nigeria*. Zaria: Tamaza Publishing Co. Ltd.

Abah, O. S. (2005) *Performing Life*. Zaria: Tamaza Publishing Co. Ltd.

Ahura, T. (1982), 'Awareness and involvement through Popular Theatre: The Ighura Experience'. *Nigeria Magazine* No.143, pp59-64.

Althusser, L. (1984), 'Ideology and Ideological Sate Apparatuses (Notes Towards an Investigation)' in Althusser, L. (Brewster, Ben and Locke Grahame trans.) (1984) *Essays on Ideology*. London: Verso Books.

Amkpa, A. (2004), *Theatre and Postcolonial Desires*. London: Routledge.

Banham, M., Gibbs, J. and Osofisan, F. (eds.) (1999) *African Theatre in Development*. Oxford: James Currey.

Boal, A. (1979), *Theatre of the Oppressed*. London: Pluto Press.

Etherton, M. (1982) *The Development of African Drama*. London: Hutchinson.

Ewu, J. (1999), 'Arts and development II. Furthering the Agenda, Ibadan' in Banham, M., Gibbs, J. and Osofisan, F. (eds.) *African Theatre in Development*. Oxford: James Currey, pp. 87-98.

Ewu, Jumai ed (2002), *Theatre for Development- a Digest of Experiences*. Vol. 12 (Parts 1+2).

Federal Ministry of Women Affairs and United Nations Development Programme (1996), *The social and Economic Status of Women in Nigeria*, Unpublished.

Freire, P. (1972), *Pedagogy of the Oppressed*. London: Penguin.

Hamrell, S. and Nordberg, O, eds. (1982), *Development Dialogue*. 1-2.

Harding, F. (1999), 'Fifteen Years Between Benue & Katsina Workshops, Nigeria' in Banham, M., Gibbs, J. and Osofisan, F. eds. (1999), *African Theatre in Development*. Oxford: James Currey, pp. 99-112.

Illah, E. (2005), 'Ochideche and Self-Empowerment: Otobi Rural Women' in Abah, O. S. (2005) *Performing Life*. Zaria: Tamaza publishing Co.

Ltd., pp.124-132.

International Human Rights Law Group (2003), *Drama and Advocacy for Voter Education in Nigeria*. Abuja: The Ragent (Printing & Publishing).

Kershaw, B. (1992), *The Politics of Performance. Radical Theatre as Cultural Intervention*. London: Routledge.

Kidd, R. and Colletta, N, eds. (1980), *Tradition for Development: Indigenous Structures and Folk Media in Non Formal Education*. Berlin: German Foundation for International Development and International Council for Adult Education.

Mike, C. & Members of the PSW (1999), 'Performance Studio Workshop. Igboelerin East' in Banham, M., Gibbs, J. and Osofisan, F. (eds.) (1999) *African Theatre in Development*. Oxford: James Currey, pp. 61-78.

Rodney, W. (1972), *How Europe Underdeveloped Africa*. Oxford, Oxford University Press.

Schechner, Richard (1988), *Performance Theory*. London: Routledge.

Srampickal, Jacob (1994), *Voice to the Voiceless*. New Delhi: Manohar.

Soyinka, W. (1993), *Art, Dialogue and Outrage*. London: Methuen.

Wa Thiongo, Ngugi (1981), *Writers in Politics*. London: Heinemann.

Wa Thiongo, Ngugi (1982), 'Women in Cultural Work: The Fate of Kamiriithu People's Theatre in Kenya' in Hamrell, S. and Nordberg, O. (eds.) *Development Dialogue*. 1-2, pp. 115-133.

Williams, R. (1977), *Marxism and Literature*. Oxford: Oxford University Press.

WIN (1982a), Newsletter. No.1 (June issue).

WIN (1982b), Memo from the Steering Committee.

* The material for this paper has come from on going research into Theatre for Development and Women's Empowerment in Nigeria funded by the Arts and Humanities Research Council (AHRC).

African Performance Review

APR

Annual Subscription Rates

Companies/orgs./institutions: (including access to the online editions)	£120
Online only	£100
Individuals: online and Print:	£50
Online only:	£30

To contribute, contact the journal's editor;

The Editor, (Dr Osita Okagbue)
Department of Drama, Goldsmiths, University of London, SE14 6NW United Kingdom. Tel: +44 (0)207 919-7581.
Email: AfTA@gold.ac.uk.

Subscription enquiries,
please contact: sales@adonis-abbey.com

Adonis & Abbey Publishers Ltd
P.O. Box 43418,
London
SE11 4XZ
United Kingdom
Tel.: +44 (0) 2077938893

Beyond the Yoruba Cosmology:
A Contestation of the Africanness of Wole Soyinka's Submission in *Myth, Literature and the African World*

Emmy Unuja Idegu (PhD)
Benue State University, Makurdi, Nigeria

Abstract

A great part of the early works of African writers and critics dealt with the issue of re-defining the African culture which, to a certain extent, was seen not to have been properly presented or represented by foreign writers. Another level of this scholarship was the response of African scholars to the attempt to universalize western culture by the West. Nevertheless, some Africans in their response to the West made postulations and generalized submissions, using a microcosm of a single African culture to stand for the whole, and thus repeating the same universalising tendency which Western scholarship had been guilty of. This paper attempts to challenge the assumed 'Africanness' of Wole Soyinka's Yoruba cosmology in *Myth, Literature and the African World*, which he uses to propose a universal African literary and tragic aesthetic.

Introduction

In every part of Africa, people of diverse origins and geographical entities and ethnic configurations are founded, bound and live together, propelled by amongst other things, their belief systems. Several instances attest to the validity of this essence of humanity, and of the relationship of the people with their past, their understandable but sometimes mysterious inexplicable worlds. Therein myth, legends, history and the like come handy in man's attempt to comprehend his immediate and remote environments.

There is probably no single subject which ethnographers, anthropologists and theatre scholars, concern themselves more than attempts to understand and interpret the belief systems of peoples of Africa and how these are reflected in their lives, (both here and hereafter) and in their works. It should be noted however, that in Africa, the men who made the greater contributions to our earlier thoughts about the

African belief systems were not themselves ethnographers; they did not know Africa and their peoples at firsthand and therefore could not have done appropriate justice to their writings about Africa. Take the age – long debate on the concept and practice, of African theatre and drama or African literature for example. The issue of Africa and its history received same skepticism from the West. At a point the entire Africans were seen as animists. To the Western world, animism was in fact an analytical system for organizing the data of African religion(s), and not a folk or operational system for organizing ritual activities and their underlying beliefs. However, animism, to put it in its simplest terms, is the attribution of soul or spirit comparable to the soul or spirit of man, to non-human animals, to plants, and even to things and abstract concepts. Paul Bohannan (1971:311). The resultant effect has always been that the facts of indigenous religion, belief systems and cosmologies lie hidden in a vast morass of misconstrued, misjudged and albeit, misunderstood theorizing. Mudimbe V. Y. cited by Margaret Thompson Drewal (1992: xiii) observes that,

> Until now, western interpreters as well as African analysts have been using categories, which depend on a Western epistemological order. Does this mean that African traditional systems of thought are unthinkable and cannot be made explicit within the framework of their own rationality?

Soyinka, W. (1976: x) thinking along this assertion also submits that,

> We black Africans have been blindly invited to submit ourselves to a second epoch of colonization - this time by a universal – humanoid abstraction defined and conducted by individuals whose theories and prescriptions are derived from the apprehension of their world and their history, their social neuroses and their value systems. It is time, clearly, to respond to his new threat.

African scholars responded to this threat in various forms, which included Negritude, Pan-Africanism and other literary and theoretical responses by Africans. Soyinka (1976: xi) asserts that,

> When ideological relations begin to deny, both theoretically and in action, the reality of a cultural entity, which we define as the African world while asserting theory even to sublimate its existence in theory, we must begin to look seriously into their political motivation.

This assertion could be seen to have propelled Soyinka (1976: xi) into his submissions in *Myth, Literature and the African World*, which he opines to be,

> ...engaged in what should be the simultaneous act of eliciting from

history, mythology and literature, for the benefit of both genuine aliens and alienated Africans, a continuing process of self – apprehension whose temporary dislocation appears to have persuaded many of its non-existence or its irrelevance in contemporary world reality.

For Soyinka, the reality of the Yoruba can most probably and conveniently be exemplified in his structured three worlds of the Living, the Dead and the Unborn.

Soyinka's Yoruba Cosmology

The Yoruba, like most African peoples, have a very rich culture. Myth plays prominent roles in the understanding of cosmic arrangements and the issue of who occupies where, in maintaining cosmic peace. Every society has myths about what it does not understand, about, if one may say, its mysteries. Yet the myths are kept nurtured by things more tangible; the recurrent events in which they are played out with greater or lesser symbolic nicety. Accompanying every set of myths, there are sets of activities that garnish the belief system of the people through which attempts are made to understand both the unknown and those mysteries of human existence.

In his treatment of the three worlds in Yoruba cosmology, Soyinka makes it clear that the gods are the final measure of eternity as humans are of earthy transience. The living does not fail to distinguish between himself and the deities, between himself and the ancestors, between the unborn and his reality, or discard his awareness of the essential gulf that lies between one area of existence and another... which must be constantly diminished by the sacrifices of the rituals, the ceremonies of appeasement to those cosmic powers which lie guardian to the gulf. Soyinka (1976: 144). This way, the three worlds (the Living the Dead and the Unborn) are constantly in a continuum of relationship as they compliment each other for cosmic tranquility. That is why, in Soyinka's Yoruba cosmology, the past belongs to the ancestors; the present belongs to the living and the future to the unborn. This could sound strange to some other cosmologies in Africa, however, to the Yoruba, these different levels have no mysteries. Soyinka (1976:149) submits that the future (the Unborn) though unknown, is nevertheless, a mystery to the Yoruba but co – existent in present consciousness.

Soyinka's presentation of the Yoruba cosmology provokes so many questions. Has Soyinka in his treatment actually captured the essence of the cosmology of the entire Yoruba people and their belief system? Can Soyinka's response to the non-African postulations as submitted in the Yoruba belief system be said to be African? How broadly African is Soyinka's submission? What are the meeting points and areas of contradictions in comparative cosmologies of other Nigerian (and African) belief systems? Is there any singularity in African worldview? How appropriate therefore can the Yoruba worldview stand for the entire African worldview?

Some scholars of Soyinka's position in *Myth, Literature and the African World* are critical of him for taking the issue of the multiplicity of cosmologies in Africa for granted. Kwame A Appiah (1992: 79) summarizes these reactions when he observes that,

> ...we should ask what leads Soyinka astray when it comes to his accounting for his cultural situation. And part of the answer must be that he is answering the wrong question. For what he needs to do is not to take an African world for granted but to take for granted his own culture – to speak not as an African but as a Yoruba and a Nigerian.

As dynamic as Appiah's submission is, even in Nigeria, a country with multidimensional cosmologies that are at times similar, yet in broad instances, antipodal to each other, a single voice representing these multiplicities, can never put forward any balanced representation. Raising a view towards this observation, Kwame A Appiah (1992:80) says that

> The right question then, is not "why Africa shouldn't take its traditions for granted?" but "why I shouldn't take mine?' the reason that Africa cannot take an African cultural or political or intellectual life for granted is that there is no such thing; there are only so many traditions with their complex relationships, and as often, their lack of any relationship to each other. Even when addressing other Africans, he can only take for granted an interest in his situation and a shred assumption that he has the right to speak from within a Yoruba cultural world. He cannot take for granted a common stock of cultural knowledge. (For this will amount to)... *a kind of Yoruba imperialism of the thought world.* (emphasis mine)

We had observed earlier the crucial role of the belief system of a people in the understanding of their cosmology. In spite of the multiplicity of African belief systems, there are meeting points. However, because of the uniqueness and distinct individual identities that seeming universality of the areas of similarity can never submerge, talking with absolutism on a matter like this amount to some level of indigenous colonialism or cultural imperialism by Soyinka.

A lot of scholars who respond to Soyinks's Africanisation of his Yoruba cosmology, at some instances, see his work from the point of view of cultural imperialism, rather than cultural influence. While cultural imperialism promotes, distinguishes, separates or even artificially injects the culture of one nation or people into another or others; in this instance, Soyinka, over other cultures in Africa, cultural influence can be seen as a process that goes on at all times between other cultures that have contact with each other. African musical traditions for instance, influenced African

American music, which in turn influenced American popular music. In cultural imperialism, it is far from the issue of influence, but a state where one culture is imposed on or dominates a great majority of other cultures.

The issue of cultural imperialism is a global phenomenon that has attracted attention for decades. At the global level, America, using her entertainment industry has received heavy criticisms. Hollywood has remained America's most vibrant tool in global cultural imperialism. Countries of the world, both the developed and the developing, have been very critical of Hollywood and its incursion on other cultures. The Indian writer, Baburo Patel (1951) cited by Toby Miller *et al* (2005:74) summarises global reactions to Hollywood when he wrote in his article, "Rape of our Heritage" about the Indian experience thus;

> The movies... pictures after pictures were sent to India that taught us to kill and steal, pictures that taught us devilry and divorce. Hollywood stripped our women of the beautiful *cholis* and *saris* and wrapped them in shirts and slacks. Hollywood turned our seashores into bedrooms of illicit romance. Hollywood robbed our men of their character and gave them guns to rob others. Hollywood ruined our homes and built clubs and dance halls on their ruins. Hollywood debauched the sanctity of our married life and glorified the illicit thrills of free love. Hollywood destroyed the philosophic fibre of the East and turned us into a frenzied mob of neurotics. Hollywood has violated our food, water, air, arts, music, culture, costumes, philosophy, life and human relations. Whatever Hollywood touched was contaminated.

This kind of sustained critique assisted in the development of a cultural imperialism thesis during the 1960s. It argued that the US, as the world's leading exporter was transferring its dominant value system to others with little or no restraints or resistance. Apart from the US, other governments and individuals have been engaged in this deliberate attempt to legitimize their culture over others. Though Soyinka's case may not be as damaging as Hollywood reported here, nevertheless, his work has had an overbearing dominance on Africa to the extent that some scholars in Africa see no reason to look inwards and study their cosmologies, falling back on the Soyinka Yoruba cosmology as all embracing. This equates what Jack Lang (1982) in Mallelart *et al* (1988:20) tags "intellectual imperialism" and cultural conquest; which according to Paolo Freire (1972:122) leads to a lack of cultural authenticity of those who are invaded. By this invasion and seeming capture of the multiplicity of cosmologies in Africa, Soyinka used his Yoruba culture to dominate the broad based scholarship on African worldview for a long time.

Select Cosmologies of Nigerian Ethnic Groups: Similarities and Contradictions with Soyinka's Yoruba Cosmolog

"African world" issues were raised by Soyinka in the text under consideration. However, because the emphasis of this paper is on Soyinka's Yoruba cosmology, let us consider the cosmologies of a few independent Nigerian ethnic nationalities in the Middle Belt Region, just one out of the six geo-political zones, for further illustration.

The Igala People

The Igala believe in the world of the Living (Ef'ile), the Dead (Efoj'egwu- inhabited by ancestors, some of which are deified as intermediary gods) and the world that is the abode of the Supreme Being, Odoba Oga'gwu- Ojo Chamachaala. The supremacy of the Supreme Being over both the Dead and the Living in Igala cosmology is unquestionable. He is Ojo; the Creator, the Father, the Protector, the Giver of all, the all-powerful. The Igalaman is always conscious of *Ojo* everywhere and in all human endeavours. He is the giver of children, hence names given to some children have *Ojo* as prefix thus; *Ojonoma* (God owns children), *Ojonimi* (God owns life), *Ojochogu* (God is medicine – or God heals) *Ojoma* (God knows), to mention just a few. Days of the week are also prefixed *Ojo*. *Ojo aladi* (Sunday), *Ojo imonde* (Monday), and so are the other days of the week. Important days also bear *Ojo*; e.g *Ojo aja* (market day). At daybreak, the Igalaman says *Ojo munwa* and at sunset he says *Ojo'du*.

These portray the prevalence of *Ojo*, who though lives very high above, is yet constantly present with man. *Ojo's* position which is the highest in the Iglaman's cosmological order is followed by the world inhabited by the Ab'egwu- the Dead, and then the Living who *J'efile* (inhabit the earth). Since the living are the lowest in the cosmological order, they live in complete obedience to *Ojo* and the ancestors who act as intermediaries between Odoba Ogagwu-*Ojo Chamachaala* and the living. Unlike Soyinka's Yoruba cosmology, the world of the unborn is of no significance in the Igalaman's understanding of his cosmological order. Emmy Idegu (1988:21).

The Idoma People.

They are in Benue State of Nigeria. Jenkeri Okwori (1998:10) summarises the Idoma cosmology when he documents that,

> The Idoma recognize the existence of an all-powerful God, *Owoicho*, who is physically separated from the earth and who can be reached through plenipotentiaries. One of his biggest plenipotentiaries is the *Aje* (earth)

and the *Oche* (who) by virtue of his being the religious head, is the *Ond' aje* (owner of the land). The *Aje* is one of the biggest manifestations of *Owoicho's* presence and it must have acquired such importance because of its life – giving force. The people depend on the land for their survival in terms of shelter, food and the place they return to when they die. Though their physical bodies return to the earth, their souls return to another level of existence, the ancestral home, where they become ancestral gods. *Owoicho* through his plenipotentiaries the *Aje* and the ancestors combine to form the religions base of the Idoma people, running their affairs and partaking in their activities to ensure the existence and the continuation of the people.

Like the Igala cosmology, the Idoma recognize the world of the living, the dead and the space occupied by *Owoicho*, the Supreme Being. But unlike the Yoruba belief system where the creation of man and woman is a combined effort of Obatala and Edumare, in the Idoma cosmology, like the Igala, *Owoicho Manchala* solely created man and woman from the earth. The God of the universe is manifested on earth because it is only through the earth that we see the mystery of *Owoicho Manchala*. Jenkeri Okwori (04-07-06).

On the world of the dead for the Idoma cosmology, Jenkeri Okwori (04-07-06) submits that if you have lived a meaningful life and you die very old, you progress into ancestorhood. Once you become an ancestor, you are deified with godly qualities and empowered by *Owoicho Manchala* to liaise with the world of the living. But on the world of the unborn he concludes that "the Idoma people do not have the concept of the unborn inhabiting a different world. Rather the ancestors can reincarnate and come out as children. Every child is believed to be a reincarnation of somebody who has died. It is more or less like coming from the ancestral world into the world of the living. Strictly speaking, we do not acknowledge the world of the unborn where children are said to come from as in the Yoruba submission".

The Bassa – Nge People.

They are a migrant group of the Nupe people (in Niger state) who live in Kogi State. Samuel Kafewo (2006) asserts that,

> Basically there are parallels in the African belief systems but they also have local peculiarities. The Bassa – Nge people believe in the world inhabited by the *Soko, the,* Supreme Being, that is God. Below Him are the smaller gods, after which are the *Akuch*i the (ancestors) then the Living that inhabit the earth. The Bassa – Nge believe *Soko* created man and He exists somewhere from where He controls all the actions of men. But for the Living to interact with *Soko,* they need to do so through the lesser gods and the ancestors. The *Akuchi* (ancestors) are believed to always hover round the living to protect them. That is why when you give somebody

water or wine, the first thing he does is to pour some on the ground appealing to the sprits of his *Akuchi* who are sometimes trapped in stones and other material forms in and around compounds.

Reacting to the issue of the place of the unborn, he admitted that the Bassa Nge have no special world for them. It is believed that every child that is born comes from some old relations that are dead. This accounts for why children are named after their dead relations. Basically the Bassa – Nge share a striking similarity of the reincarnation act with the Idoma. However, like the Igala and the Idoma people, the Bassa – Nge have no space for the unborn in their cosmic arrangement.

The Birom People.

They are in Plateau State. They believe in the world inhabited by *Dagwi*, the Supreme Being, the earth inhabited by the living and the space where the dead (ancestors) reside. Apart from their believe in *Vu Vwel* (the spirit of the dead), there are other smaller spirits called *Bevwo Vwel* and *Cheng* or *Chit*, who are part of *Vu Vwel*. While *Bevwo Vwel* are unharmful, untouchable and unhelpful, holy and good and from *Dagwi* (God), *Cheng* or *Chit* are categorized as evil spirits and they inhabit trees, thickets and isolated habitats (Erivwo in Edith Ihekweazu ed. 1985:98). *Cheng* or *chit*, are nevertheless also seen as guardian spirits of the village, protecting the people from harm. The spirits have a relationship with the living that they visit often. The Birom people do not bother to explain how the spirits came into being. Rather they claim that they see and know that spirits exist while they are not able to explain the precise connection between *Chit* and *Dagwi*, but they nevertheless acknowledge *Dagwi* as the Supreme Being who has power over *Chit* and that without *Dagwi's* permission *Chit* could not punish human beings who go wrong. Edith Ihekweazu (1985:99). The Birom cosmology therefore obviously acknowledges three distinct worlds; the world of the living, the dead and the world inhabited by *Dagwi*. The Soyinka Yoruba world of the unborn to the Birom is nonexistent.

The Ngas (Angas) People.

They are in Plateau State. They believe that *Nen*, the Supreme Being, created human beings and every other thing on earth including *Zigwol Rit* and *Zigwol Bis* (ancestral sprits). While Zigwol Bis opposes *Nen* by acting as a reservoir of wickedness from where witches derive their power, *Zigwol Rit* furthers *Nen's* benevolence and divine purpose for man. The Ngas are, according to Erivwo (1985:104), "satisfied to believe and know that there are spirits and divinities, that some of them are good while others are bad and aggressive, that they emanate from the spirit world to disclose themselves to men, that in some ways they function as ministers and ambassadors of *Nen*. By the Ngas cosmology, three worlds are acknowledged; the world of the living, the dead (spirits) and the space occupied by *Nen*. Again, Soyinka's Yoruba crucial world of the unborn has no space here.

The Taroh People.

Like the Birom and the Ngas, the Taroh are in Plateau State. They believe that *Inan* is the Supreme Being and creator of all. The divinities, spirits, ancestors and the living are all subject to Him. He solely created them all. The humans offer sacrifices to the diversities, spirits and ancestors who thereafter relay these to *Inan*. To attain ancestorhood, Erivwo (1985: 109) submits that,

> When a hero in the clan dies, he is remembered in the clan for many generations. Libation is poured in remembrance of him at his grave every year. If as the years roll by, his name is getting out of the mind of the clan folk, the head of the clan gets trees planted round a hut built at the place to facilitate his worship. In this way the clan keeps in touch with him and obtains protection, guidance, and blessings from him. In this way, the people are assured (or assure themselves) of receiving his help in times of trouble whenever they need his aid.

The Taroh cosmology, like others treated thus far ascribes creation to *Inan* the Supreme Being, who alone does the act of the creation of man, woman and everything. Here also, Soyinka's Yoruba world of the unborn is of no consequence.

In his analysis of the Yoruba cosmology, their gods and their different responsibilities, Soyinka's submission is contradicted by these cosmologies in the Middle Belt zone of Nigeria. For instance, according to Soyinka's Yoruba belief system, Obatala is the creator of man. Obatala made man out of clay. He molded man and woman and he asked Olodumare to put the breath of life into them. Ullie Beier (1980:14). This position was earlier shared by Soyinka (1976:15), by whose Yoruba world view, the making of man and woman is the combined responsibility of Obatala (who molds) and Olodumare (who supplies the breath). Soyinka (1976:140) refers to Edumare (another variance for Olodumare) as the Supreme Deity. Where in Soyinka's Yoruba three worlds does Edumare inhabit? Soyinka's Edumare who according to him is supreme, yet needs Obatala to make man whole, contradicts the belief systems treated above that have the Supreme Being as the Creator of man and woman without any complementary role of any other god.

We have not even considered the Igbo, Hausa, Ijaw, Kalabari, Efik, Ibibio, Urhobo, Tiv, and the over three hundred other ethnic nationalities and their diverse cosmologies in Nigeria; not to talk of other countries of

Africa. From the Igala, Idoma, Bassa – Nge, Birom, Ngas, Taroh, cosmologies referred to, their collective similarities with the Yoruba cosmology evidently is in two worlds; the world of the living and the dead. These collective six (C 6) share the supremacy of the Supreme Being and attest to Him as the sole creator of everything including objects and substances from which the Yoruba gods are said to have emerged. The (C 6) standing in for several other cultures, either rejects absolutely, or de-emphasizes, the world of the unborn which nonetheless, occupies a fundamental position in Soyinka's Yoruba cosmology. So crucial is the Yoruba world of the unborn that Soyinka (1976:144) admits succinctly that life, present life, contains within it manifestations of the ancestral, the living and the unborn. All are vitally within the intimations and effectiveness of life, beyond mere abstract conceptualization. Adeoti G.R (2006) agrees with Soyinka when the explains that,

> When Obatala molds the human form, Olodumare gives the breath before you can be born. But why this process is completed you will then go to a place where you choose your destiny. Whatever type of destiny you choose determines who you become after you are born. So even before birth, there is a level of consciousness which Soyinka terms the unborn.

As acceptable as this whole process may be to the Yoruba, it does not fit into a number of belief systems even within the confines of Yoruba neighbours in Nigeria. The similarities between the Yoruba cosmology and the C 6 as one may argue for other ethnicities in Nigeria (or Africa), do not nonetheless give credence to using one of the several cosmologies as the singular platform to coin an African worldview. For as similar in origin, functions and responsibilities as Soyinka's gods in the Yoruba myth he popularizes are, Soyinka himself knows Ogun, Obatala, Sango, and the a thousand and one fragmented gods in the Yoruba mythology possess their unique individualities. The concept of the world of the unborn, and its irrelevance in the C 6, for instance, is a great absurdity in Soyinka's attempt to carve the entire African world from the peculiar Yoruba perspective.

Soyinka's response was principally, amongst other reasons, to challenge the intellectual arrogance of the West at a point. He was contesting a European attempt to globalize their culture, as one may add his reaction to a dominant intellectual debate of the period he wrote. Dapo Adelugba (2006) rightly attests that,

> The first thing we must all accept is that Soyinka was not writing for all times, a theoretical paper. He was deliberating on the essences of African life and culture. You have to study that against the background of the dominance of European thought in the intellectual world. Soyinka's position then and now is that Europe has an intellectual culture but they are not the only holders of the key to intellectual culture. Intellectual culture can be found in other societies also. Soyinka used the Yoruba

paradigm but his aim was perhaps to reach out to a bigger African paradigm. I do not think the easy does that, but at least, it makes suggestions about the validity to the African belief systems and used the Yoruba, in my view, as an example rather than the African absolute truth. Because the Yoruba may after all not be rigidly homogenous, the question now arises as to whether Soyinka's submission covers the entire Yoruba territory. He is only one man making a proposition, basing his proposition on his personal experience of what he has comically described as the "Ijegba" culture.

Soyinka's deliberate down – playing of the place of the Supreme Being as the singular creator and the Almighty seen by the C 6 cosmologies may after all, be a reflection of his personal belief system superimposed on the Yoruba cosmology which he exported as African. Dapo Adelugba (2006) in his admission says that inevitably,

> ...each person has a point of view. We cannot run away from the fact that <u>Soyinka's apprehension of Yoruba cosmology has been filtered through his own understanding, his own growth, his own experiences and his own eventual belief system</u>. Soyinka is a Yoruba man who wants to explain everything to himself in the way he understands not in the way the people of the precious generations saw it. But the way he sees it (emphasis mine).

Though Soyinka's theoretical and mythical thrust was a response to a civilization that assumed and ascribed to itself absolutism in intellectual discourse, he may also consequently be seen in the same light as those he lampoons. In his reaction to Ali Mazrui's "Africa: A Triple Heritage", for instance, Soyinka (1991: 20) critiques Mazrui's documentary as,

> A series, which we were informed, was designed to redress the appalling ignorance and misrepresentation of a vast continent ended up as yet another expensive propaganda for furthering the claims of the racial – religious superiority of <u>two other structures of human superstitions</u> which were imparted into Africa and forced down the throats of its peoples, and with an unembarrassed bias towards Islam (emphasis mine)

For Soyinka, because the two belief systems treated by Mazrui that he refers to here-(Christianity and Islam) do not share Soyinka's personal belief system, he refers to them as "two other structures of human superstitions". To subsume the two principal faiths (Christianity and Islam) as mere "human superstitions" exemplifies Soyinka's obvious ignorance of Mazrui's claims and his arrant theoretical and scholarly arrogance. Soyinka's reaction to Mazrui's presentation was rekindled in Soyinka (2006) where he took up again, on a religious activity, this time around, the Christian faith. Commenting on a great evangelistic revival in a restoration crusade organized by the United Congress of Mbaise Christians during which over one hundred shrines in the land were destroyed after their worshippers got converted to the Christian faith, Soyinka (2006:13) referring to the organizers as "Christian pyromaniacs" rhetorically asks,

> Have you deployed trained archaeologists, sociologists, ethnologists, indeed, pharmacologists or whatever to these shrines, those who have the training to discern whether the target of destruction may, or may not contain objects of archival value? Have you taken the trouble to separate the wheat from the chaff? Do you consider it part of <u>our collective responsibility</u> to ensure that this is done? (emphasis mine)

Considering Soyinka's questions with his background, his focus is far from mere aesthetic values of the destroyed objects. The objects destroyed in the said shrines were not ordinary sculptors that could be put in museums. The same way Soyinka may never subscribe to the excavation of the shrine of Ogun, his patron god, into the national archive for any reason, even if the best professionals he listed in his rhetorical questions were on ground to supervise it. The objects had graduated from the ordinary aesthetic objects Soyinka calls them here to spiritually potent items. In this instance, not the kind of professionals listed by Soyinka except the evangelists who "have the training to discern" the spiritual implications of those shrines would have sufficed. As a scholar of the Yoruba cosmology and belief system, Soyinka should have known that what the United Congress of Mbaise Christians did was a spiritual cleansing dictated by the belief system within which framework they operated. As an advocate of the Yoruba belief system and a cross-cultural scholar Soyinka should accord respect to other belief systems and their adherents beyond his uncomplimentary reference to them as "Christian pyromaniacs", people endowed with the morbid propensity to set things on fire, and rather unjustifiably.

For the Mbaise outing, Soyinka advocates for "our collective responsibility". However, in his vocal Africanization of the Yoruba cosmology, he forgot to apply the same principle. He ought to have carefully studied other cosmologies across Africa, brought into the limelight their meeting points and thereafter based his submission on the collective consideration to arrive at the African worldview. It is this identifiable individualism in Soyinka's approach that Kwame A. Appiah, (1992: 83) summaries when he says that,

> Soyinka, the individual, a Nigerian outside the traditional, more certain world of his Yoruba ancestors, struggles with the Soyinka who experiences the loss of that world, of those gods of whom (which) he speaks with such love and longing. Once again, the "I" seeks to escape the persistent and engulfing "we".

Soyinka has over time, exhibited the "I" than a "we"-conscious intellectual and theorist on several levels of study. He theorizes and writes most often, without taking into due consideration his readers. He once confessed that he writes,

> ...in the firm believe that there must be at least a hall full of people who are sort of on the same wave length as mine in every stratum of society and there must be at least a thousand people who are able to feel the same way as I do about something. (Yemi Ogunbiyi, 1981:39).

The "hall full of people" in which a thousand of them will reason on "the same wave length" with Soyinka, may, most probably not even be found in Europe, not to talk of Africa his base.

Conclusion

This paper has attempted to appraise Soyinka's Yoruba "African worldview" in his *Myth, Literature and the African World* laying emphasis on the Yoruba cosmology and as it relates either in agreement or divergence with select six cosmologies from one, out of the six geo-political zones of Nigeria. While acknowledging the "Africanness" in Soyinka's response to European civilization, his theorized Yoruba view as an "African worldview" is suspect. A lot of questions will keep on arising. The summary of the questions can be found in Kwame A. Appiah (1992:80) when he asks,

> What has Yoruba cosmology, the preoccupation of the first lecture of *Myth Literature and the African World*, to do with African literature; it is not enough to answer that Yoruba cosmology provides both the characters and the mythic resonance of some African drama – notably, of course, Soyinka's. This (Soyinka's submission) is no answer for the Akan writer or reader who is more familiar with Ananse than Esu – Elegba as trickster, and who had no more obligations to Ogun than he does to Vishnu.

Therefore, one man's theorization need not be held as a kind of absolute for all parts of Africa. Even within the African continent as other scholars and philosophers have pointed out, there are lots of variables even in belief systems, cosmologies and so on. The Yoruba cosmology cannot even be wholly valid in the entire Yorubaland, not to talk of Igalaland and the other parts of Nigeria and the entire Africa. Dapo Adelugba (2006), opines that,

> ...it is not valid to say that one part (the Yoruba cosmology) is equal to or greater than the whole (other cosmologies in Africa), but one part can be an illustration of the whole. Soyinka's essay seems to be an illustration rather than a law – given essay. It is just an individual apprehension of a greater phenomenon. We also can go into that stream and come up with

our own individual interpretations.

We live in a world that is irreversibly plural where culture is concerned. Nevertheless, a harmonious African panoramic view of cosmologies by sharing what is convergent and in mutual respect for what is divergent would have enriched Soyinka's submission. This paper's argument is based on the premise that the significance of any African cosmology differs from people to people and culture to culture, and that cultural identity (exemplified for instance, in the C 6) is the standard bearer of an alternative to the cultural imperialism of Soyinka.

References

Appiah, Kwame A. (1992), *In My Father's House: Africa in the Philosophy of Culture*, Oxford, Oxford University Press.

Bohannan, Paul (1971), *Social Anthoyloglgy*, London, Holt Rinehart and Winston.

Drewal ,Margaret Thompson (1992) *Yoruba Ritual: Performers, Play, Agency,* Bloomington, Indiana University press.

Freire, Paulo (1972), *Pedagogy of the Oppressed*, Harmondsworth, Penguin.

Idegu, Emmy (1988), "The Socio – Cultural Significance of *Ogani* festival among the Igala People" MA Drama Dissertation, Department of English and Drama, A.B.U. Zaria unpublished

Ihekweazu, Edith (ed) (1985), *Readings in African Humanities: Traditional and Modern Cultures,* Enugu, Fourth Dimension publishers.

Mattelart, Michele et al (1998), *Theories of Communication,* London,Sage

Ogunbiyi, Yemi, (ed) (1981). *Drama and Theatre in Nigeria: A Critical Source Book,* Lagos, Nigeria Magazine.

Okwori,Jenkeri(1998), *Ije: The Performance Traditions of the Idoma,* Zaria, Bright Printing Press

Soyinka, Wole. (1976), *Myth, Literature. and the African World,* London, Cambridge University Press.

Soyinka, Wole. (1991), *The Credo of Being and Nothingness* Ibadan, Spectrum.

Soyinka, Wole. (2006), *Forget the Past, Forfeit the Future,* Zaria, A.B.U. Press.

Miller,T et al (2005), *Global Hollywood (2),* London, British Film Institute

Interviews on 04-07-06 at the Ahmadu Bello University, Zaria,

Adelugba Dapo – Professor of Theatre Arts on Sabbatical to the Department of Theatre and Performing Arts. Ahmadu Bello University (A.B.U), Zaria.

Okwori Jenkeri Zakari (Associate Professor of Theatre and

Performing, Arts) A.B.U. Zaria.

Kafewo, Samuel (PhD), visiting Senior Lecturer to the University of Cape Coas Ghana.

G. R. Adeoti (PhD), on Sabbatical with the Department of English and Literary Studies, A.B.U, Zaria.

I remain very grateful to Professor Dapo Adelugba and the above persons for granting me audience.

Through Other Eyes and Voices:
Women in *Koteba* and *Mmonwu* Performances

Osita Okagbue
Goldsmiths, University of London, United Kingdom

Abstract

In many indigenous African performances while a sizeable number of the characters and the majority of the spectators are female, only men and male actors organise and perform in these theatrical performances. This observation was particularly obvious in the *Koteba* of the Bamana of Mali and *Mmonwu* performances of the Igbo of Nigeria which I studied recently.

This paper's main argument is that theatrical performances are very much part of the cultural and social processes of society and they are therefore implicated in the politics of identity and its representation in society. Thus, the marginalisation of women in most spheres of public life in Bamana and Igbo societies is graphically reflected in the fact that in the two performances, women remain on the sidelines, on the receiving end of male articulations of male and other identities. Women's views, their identities and the power to occupy and thus speak from the public domain and space are denied and usurped by the dominant male 'Other' who uses this power to maintain hold on power. The paper concludes therefore that very often a theatrical performance is a good indicator and a reflection of the culture or society from which it originates, and that perhaps changing the mechanics and dynamics of performance may be the way to change the mechanics and dynamics of society.

Introduction

On an evening in late July 2004, a steady stream of people could be seen animatedly making their way towards the centre of Markala, a town a few kilometres away from Segou in Mali; they were all heading towards a walled compound, which was the *ton* compound. The *ton* is the Bambara name for the youth association which exists in every Bamana village or town. The crowd was excited because it was assembling to watch a performance of the popular comic satires being staged by the town's *koteba-ton* – the theatre group within the *ton*. What was firstly noticeable about this stream of potential audience was its composition: it comprised mainly women and children, and just a few young men. But significant by their absence were grown up men, especially the elders, who (we had been told) are the most socially and politically powerful group in Bamana society.

That the elders keep away from the performances is understandable and will be explored later in this paper. The stream of spectators soon filled up the audience space within the walled compound; some sat on few chairs which had been provided by the *ton* members, some had brought their own chairs along with them, while the rest found themselves vantage viewing positions. As soon as the spectators had settled in their respective places, the drummers (five in number) emerged from the changing room located down stage right playing the customary entrance music. Together with the *bamuko* dance, this opening section is called the *kotebadon*; the drummers were followed immediately by a motley group of performers/dancers who wore an assortment of costumes. They danced in a single file once round the slightly elevated stage before turning in the direction of the audience to acknowledge them. The latter responded by clapping and whooping loudly. The dancers engaged the audience in a comic banter before retreating into the dressing room, while the musicians made their way to a bench which had been reserved for them downstage right. After a while, the drummers began a new beat and tune which, since the song was intended to indicate the skit that was to follow, the audience immediately picked up and joined in. As this song and mime were going on, four of the dancers who had retreated to the dressing room after the introduction emerged and their entrance threw the entire audience into hilarious laughter because they had re-emerged as a family of four – Koke (husband), Mariamoufin (first wife), Nyebaje (second wife) and Jeneba (daughter). The family entered the stage and walked across to greet the Dugutigi (village head) who sat upstage centre. The cause of the laughter was the fact that the three women in the family were, in fact, performed by male actors; thus, the incongruity of male bulging and rippling muscles struggling to be contained and showing through female gowns and dresses, and the combined shrilly voices and 'feminine' mannerisms of the actors were too comic for words (Fig 1). The *Kote-tlon* satiric theatre of the Bamana is an all male performance. It was also even more striking that the actors were all men given that the theme to be explored in this skit – two wives in a polygamous marriage competing for the affection of their husband – was one which concerned women more than it did men. It was female behaviour and attitudes more than those of the men which were under scrutiny.

Fig. 1 Nyebaje (Moussa Diakhite) and Mariamoufin

In the first sketch, Koke has two women, Mariamoufin (first wife) and Nyebaje as the second. Mariamoufin is presented as the Bamana male's ideal woman – she is obedient and submissive to her husband even though he treats her very badly when he marries his second wife, Nyebaje. The latter has more modern and radical ideas about womanhood and her role. Nyebaje has strong views about things and insists on being heard; she is interested in her looks and well-being, boldly asserts that she is not the 'cooking or cleaning type of wife', and besides, she manages to get her husband, Koke, to do what she wants. She, as should be expected, is not a favourite of the audiences because she goes against the norm and threatens the *status quo* by what is presented as her outrageous behaviour. Because of this, she is as expected the one to lose out in the polygamous battle of the wives, while her co-wife, Mariamoufin, is praised and eventually reinstated as the favourite wife, having earlier been sent packing to her parents by the besotted Koke. Koke, in spite of his wrong judgements and bungles, ends up having the best of both worlds - he is the love interest of both women at different times in the play and all through no attempt is made to present him as the fickle-minded fool that he really is. The shows are framed in such a way that it is the women who are on trial, with one being used as a comparative foil for the other, while Koke's behaviour and antics are never scrutinised or judged. The second sketch deals with Koke and Jeneba, his daughter by Mariamoufin. Koke, having been abandoned temporarily by his two wives still has Jeneba to keep house for him. He entrusts her with the care of the home, especially with looking after his flock of beloved chickens. But all that Jeneba desires is to escape from this dreary village life and the domination of her father with her lover, Wankyu, who had recently returned from Peking (Beijing). Again, because she is seen as not accepting her designated place in the social order by trying to disrupt the father-daughter relationship or bidding to escape her socially ascribed role, Jeneba is presented as a lazy, naïve daydreamer who disobeys her father in order to please her boyfriend who, the spectators are convinced, was going to take her for a ride. Either way, she is only dreaming to escape from her father's exploitative authority into that of her lover. In no way is she conceived or presented as being capable of a life without being under the controlling influence of a man. Even her dream of escaping to China is presented as a threat to the social order and it is made to fail so she remains stuck at home attending to her father's needs and demands. The play's ending is deliberately left ambiguous, with Jeneba still on stage as her father and her lover pummel each other off stage. The spectators do not even remember her as they wildly cheer the two men off.

Similarly, the Enemma festival performances which I watched in Nkpor in Nigeria between 1993 and 1997 began for our team of researchers in the compound which the Ochammili group was using as its base. When we got to the place the musicians were already playing and some dancers were dancing round the place in the traditional *icho mmonwu* routine (this is the preliminary dance in which non-masked members of a performance troupe search for their masquerades) As we waited and watched the dancers, the group's Onuku (the Fool) masquerade emerged from the dressing room and directly proceeded to chase all the young boys around and whoever he caught he humped or simulated copulating with them. After the Onuku, came a beautiful maiden masquerade, later identified as Adamma (Beautiful Daughter), came out from the dressing room escorted by her male non-masked guide. She was dressed as a young girl in very shiny yellow costume, a red hand bag and lots of jewels around her neck and on her hair. She was very shy and would not lift her face to look at people, even when they gave her money to dance, she did so with her eyes turned away, sometimes covering her face with a little fan which she held in her right hand. She was acting the coy young woman. As soon as Onuku saw her dancing, he made for her and began trying to copulate with her, she for her part desperately protecting herself by crossing her legs and covering her genitals with her fan and handbag. The last pair to emerge from the dressing room was Nna Mmuo and Nne Mmuo, Adamma's parents. Like her daughter, Nne Mmuo was very reserved and coy in the way she carried herself, walking very demurely beside her husband, the latter reaching out to put a protective hand around her and fanning her when she danced. Unlike her daughter, Nne Mmuo wore wrapper and a blouse with elaborate head-tie. She had beads around her neck, and bangles made from elephant tusks on her wrists and ankles – the bangles and rich cloth symbolise that she is the wife of a wealthy man. Her movements and gestures, like Adamma's, were very graceful and feminine. When we eventually got to the village square where the festival was taking place, there were other family groups with similar types of characters, some were already performing when we arrived, while others came after our group. There were other mothers, daughters, flirtatious *agbogho mmuo* characters, female traders, a white European District Officer and his wife. Thus, the Enemma festival performance, like the Igbo masquerade theatre which it is a part of, had female and male characters. But significantly all the actors in the festival performances were men and are usually so in most other instances of Igbo masking theatre. The reason for this is that the *Mmonwu* cult which is responsible for all masking in Nkpor is a males-only society whose members are admitted through an initiation called *ima mmuo*. Only initiated Nkpor males are authorized to take part in the masking theatre as actors, musicians and dancers (although in some Igbo masking traditions women are allowed to participate in the theatre as dancers or in some instances they are permitted to sing).

Although different in many ways, a major feature which *Koteba* and *Mmonwu* theatre forms have in common is the exclusion of women as either performers or active participants in the theatre-making process. One often wonders why this male only participation exists in *Kote-tlon* (the satiric comedies) and *Mmonwu*, given that these two are the dominant indigenous performance forms of the Bamana of Mali and the Igbo of Nigeria, respectively. This exclusion of women and girls from the theatre-making process is even more surprising since women very often make up a sizeable proportion of the spectators for *Mmonwu* and *Koteba* performances. In fact, for the *Koteba* satiric sketches (*kote-tlon*) in particular, women are often in the majority in the audience as was the case at the shows I watched. And in Igbo culture, although they scream and run away when they see or are approached by a masquerade, women still are well represented in the audiences of *Mmonwu* performances in Nkpor, and in deed in all instances of masking theatre all over Igboland, even though they may not sit or stand in the front row.

In this paper, I intend to show that it is not by accident that women are excluded as actors or direct agents in the theatre making process in these two theatre traditions – their participation is peripheral in both. In the *Koteba*, although it can be claimed that women are part of the masked performances, being positioned within the concentric rings made up of lines of performers, and also singing some of the narrative songs for the *Sogo Bo* (the puppets), they still are not allowed to put on a mask and perform any of the characters, just as in the *Mmonwu* theatre. The key argument here is that a theatre form is always interwoven and implicated in the cultural fabric and socio-political structures and processes of the society from which it originates or in which it exists. And to understand this performance-society relationship, it is necessary to consider a host of interrelated factors within Bamana and Igbo societies. Key issues to consider are: the control and use of public and private spaces, the politics of articulating, negotiating and expressions of individual and shared identities, theatre as social action and part of the social process, the politics of power and social control. Knowledge of how these interrelated issues play out in Bamana and Igbo cultures should throw some light on the fact of women's exclusion in the two theatre traditions.

According to Victor Turner, cultures 'are most fully expressed in and made conscious of themselves in their ritual and theatrical performances' (in Appel and Schechner, 1990: 1). That is to say that each culture generates performance types which are expressive, as well as part of its social processes, and through performance, Turner adds, 'the central meanings, values and goals of a culture are seen "in action", as they shape and explain behavior' (1). Through theatre and performances one is able to glimpse the complex patterns of social intercourse between people within society, and one is also able to have intimations about the social processes and historical movements and cultural shifts that a society has experienced or is going through. Wherever it is made, the theatre or performance, as Maria Shevtsova points out, 'vibrates with the movement of its society' (1993: viii-ix).

Bamana and Igbo societies are patriarchal and so men have overriding cultural, social and political power. And quite often, in most matters relating to public life, men are deferred to by women, irrespective of age, intellectual and material ability - this means that in both cultures a boy ranks above his mother in social standing, and if he has a sister, she is further down in the social hierarchy. But among the men, however, especially in Bamana society, the elderly males are the group highest placed and as such they are the ones who control most social processes. Because of this, they are deferred to in all matters, whether public and private, by the younger men and the women. The implication of this is that women seem to have very little or no direct political or public power in Bamana and Igbo societies as they are often denied visibility and agency in the public domain. This dominance by elderly males in Bamana society and males in general in Igbo culture is reflected in every aspect of life in both contexts, in the privacy of the home, as well as in but more especially in the communal square, the public arena where important political and social decisions are made.

For the Bamana, the dominance of the elderly males has led to the need in the young men to use the *koteba-ton* to develop comic satires which attack and make fun of the elders. Although every young person of both sexes joins the *ton*, membership between males and females differ, for while male members can remain members until well into their forties and early fifties, women cease being members once they are married or once they reach the age of twenty-five. It is very obvious that the theatre, the *kote-tlon* in particular, is the main avenue and instrument through which the anger and dissatisfaction of the youth with the excessive power of the headmen and elders are expressed. According to Brink (1978), the power of the elders in controlling land and jobs, as well as in determining when the young men got married and became accepted as full men, produced 'latent contradictions' and tensions in the relations between elders and the often sexually and economically frustrated young males. The frustration, Kerr points out, is responsible for 'the prominence of satire on sexual themes, aimed at unfaithful wives, impotent old men and cuckolds' (1995: 5).

There are three types of *Koteba* performances - the masquerade performances which are held at the annual festival in the communal square, the non-masked satiric sketches which can be performed anywhere and at any time of the year, and the *Sogo Bo*, the puppetry performances. A major difference between the three types of performances is that while the masquerade and puppet performances usually take place during the day, the comic satires are performed at night. Another difference is that while the masked performances are concerned with sacred themes in which Bamana ancestral and folk heroes, deities and spirits feature, the satiric sketches deal with human characters and their themes are secular and social. The *kote-tlon*, as already pointed above, is the major means through which Bamana young males are able to challenge the authority and power of their male elders. In fact, the satiric sketches are the only theatre performances in Bamana culture devoted to and often used effectively as instruments and contexts for social criticism. However, while the female members of the *koteba-ton* take part in the masquerade performances which, by their very nature, are strong affirmations of the *status quo*), and while they can sing or dance in the *Sogo Bo*, it is significant that their involvement is peripheral. As dancers or chorus members they usually occupy the outer circles of the concentric rings of the *koteba* spatial structure; but they never wear masks or manipulate the puppets. The satiric comedies are a different matter altogether as they are not even allowed on the stage let alone perform in the sketches. This exclusion is very significant given that a high proportion of the characters are female and the themes explored are those which involve women. Themes and ideas explored range from representations of feminine characteristics, expected roles and responsibilities in society, and those who conform receive approbation while those who deviate or challenge these expected roles are highly disapproved of. Examples of comic/satiric sketches in the *Kote-tlon* repertory include 'The Unfaithful Wife', 'A Polygamous Husband and His Two Wives', 'The Father, the Daughter and Her Lover', 'The Blind Man, His Wife and The Leper' etc.

The other major group who are the butt of the comic sketches are the dominant elderly males and their attempts to keep their firm grip on society; in the plays they are often undermined and upstaged either by devious and scheming women such as the husband who is pulled around and manipulated by his two wives which made him look extremely stupid in the play on polygamy. The same character became the father in the second sketch in which he is pitted against a stubborn and love-struck daughter and an apparently resourceful, modern and 'progressive' thinking young man, Wank-yu, who returns to the village from Peking and promptly seduces the man's daughter, Jeneba, by promising to take her with him to China. The young girl, to impress her lover, kills and cooks one of her father's precious fowls. As the young man tucks into the meal he is challenged by the enraged father, but the younger man proceeds to teach the latter a lesson in *karate* and *kung-fu*, one of the skills he had learnt while in China. In both sketches, the old men are made to look ridiculous, while the younger men, and only occasionally the women, are triumphant.

The sketches, apart from being a means of publicly taking on the elders and playfully keeping the women in check, are also contexts for general social critique and cultural reappraisal. For the young males who, for an extended period of time in their lives, are under the authority and control of their fathers, the sketches enable them to register their dissatisfaction with the *status quo* and sometimes to seriously challenge the authority and dominance of the elders. But at times, however, it just enables them to let off steam; it gives them a public space from and a voice with which to express their displeasure; unfortunately, this means of speaking out is not also available to their female counterparts who, it seems, are denied this social and cultural right of publicly expressing their dissatisfaction. Experientially, they have their gender roles and identities defined and their lives practically run by their fathers or uncles, and theatrically, their feminine identities and female roles are represented on stage exclusively by their brothers and male cousins. This is partly so because they lose their membership of the *ton* much earlier than their male counterparts, but mainly because the patriarchal social system under which they live ensures that the *kote-tlon* performances are exclusive to the male members of the *koteba-ton* – that is, that while they can take part in the masquerade shows, they are not allowed to act in the satires. Either way, there seems to be a closing of ranks among the men when it comes to who can or can not use this public forum as a weapon to express their dissatisfactions or to challenge the *status quo*. As a result, one major instrument of critical social and self-evaluation in Bamana society, the satiric comedies, is not available to women. It was not surprising that members of the *koteba-ton* in Markala, whose performance I watched, had never given any thought to the exclusion of women and most of them were genuinely taken aback when they were asked about it. Surprisingly, however, the female members of the audience on the night who were asked about the situation, incidentally, had not given it much thought either, with many of them maintaining that it was not an issue for them.

In Nkpor masking area, women are not even allowed to see a mask costume when it is not in use, let alone touch it. Even when they've donated materials for the costumes, these are out of bounds once they are designated masquerade paraphernalia – sometimes, these materials can be reclaimed by the female donors after the performance, but they are not allowed near such materials while they are still in use. The major means of exclusion in some masquerade zones in Igboland is through initiation (*ima mmonwu*) which is only open to male children of between the ages of eight and twelve. But even in zones where there are no initiations, taking part in the masquerade theatre as a performer is not open to women and the men do all they can to maintain the mystery, (mystique) while keeping the expressive privileges of masking well out of reach of women. One of the oaths that young boys take at the end of their initiation into the cult enjoins them never to reveal the content of the initiation to their mothers or sisters and any female relatives; they are especially enjoined to keep the myth of the masquerade characters as dead ancestors and spirits returned to the world of the living intact. In fact, men in Igbo society, including young initiated boys, boast about masking as something that makes them greater than their mothers or gives them social advantage and power over them. The expression, *ife nji ka nnem,* encapsulates this sense of superiority and privilege which Igbo men feel and have over women. Thus, when asked Igbo men never acknowledge that the masked figures are disguised male actors pretending to be ancestors or other characters.

Given that the masquerade theatre is the main theatre form of Igbo culture, it is easy to understand the significance of this advantage. So, the question therefore has to be why a sizeable population in Igbo society does not have any access whatsoever to this means of artistic and cultural expression. As in the *Koteba* performances, female characters are as many as male ones in the *Mmonwu* performances, and also, as in the *Koteba*, *Mmonwu* theatre often uses satire to subject aspects of society, human behaviour and relationships to scrutiny, censor or praise. The fact that issues explored in the masquerade theatre divide equally between female and male concerns – the satiric Ayaka and Osonigwe night masquerades in Nkpor sing about men as well as about women - highlights the fact that these issues are only presented from only the male perspective. However, this fact seems to be glossed over by both men and women and, as was the case in Mali, when the male *Mmonwu* performers in Nkpor were asked to explain why women were not allowed to wear masks or perform in central positions in the theatre, they too were surprised that such a question was being raised for it had seemed natural to them and the women did not overly complain either. It was not until it was pointed out to them that it was a denial of the right to speak or respond to criticism as the men are able to do when they are caricatured or attacked in a sketch that some grudgingly acknowledged the implication of the exclusion. But the advocates of tradition among them, however, refused to see it as a problem and gave reasons which ranged from the assumption that women were not interested (a view surprisingly supported by a poll of some of the women themselves), to the view that masking is physically too demanding for the female physique and sometimes too messy for their 'delicate feminine sensibilities'. One of the main reasons why the masquerade theatre evolved, to serve as an instrument of social control with women being one of the target groups that needed to be controlled, was mentioned by only one Nkpor elder. It was logical, therefore, this elder argued, to deny such a group access to this mechanism of social control and for its secrets to be kept from them.

By making masking a semi-sacred activity, and by presenting the characters as dead ancestors returned to interact with their living descendants or as spirits of things and deities thereby giving these characters/actors attributes of the sacred, the Igbo male cult is able to claim that its activity had been ordained by the gods from the beginning of time. This also gives so much power to the actors to criticize whoever they wish to criticize without any fear of reprimand or challenge, especially from the women or non-initiates who have neither a say nor the power to use this instrument or art of representation. The almost religious and cultural setting in which the masking theatre exists in both Bamana and Igbo societies ensures that once in character, the actor can and does get away with a lot of the things done or said during a performance. But while any male person can answer back directly and in person or in extreme cases he can put on a mask to challenge the actor's viewpoint, a woman can do neither.

Politics of Representation in Bamana and Igbo Cultures

The central issue being explored here is that of representation and self-presentation in Bamana and Igbo societies; but it is also about the structures of power and the kinds of relationships they engender in both societies. As already pointed out at the beginning of this essay, both Bamana and Igbo societies are patriarchal, which means that women are subjected, marginalized and disenfranchised in a lot of ways. It also means that ideas of what is good or bad, right or wrong, beautiful or ugly are very often determined and reinforced by men. This implies that ideas of what constitutes the collective identity of the group, as well the individual identities of constituent members and sections of the society are also set, monitored and controlled by men. It is obvious then that the question of female subjection, representation and mis-representation characteristic of patriarchal systems applies in these two cultures.

The concern of this paper is the fact of the theatrical representation of women by men in Igbo and Bamana cultures; thus, Butler's (1990) argument that gender and sexuality are inherently performative could be relevant here. Also relevant in this context is Simone de Beauvoir's famous assertion that 'one is not born a woman, but rather becomes one' (1973: 301). If one were to agree with de Beauvoir and Butler, gender therefore is something the individual becomes through learning and continued performance of a set of culturally determined and approved acts and behaviours. This certainly is interesting, not only because it destabilizes the seemingly fixed binary notion of gender in society, but also because it highlights the theatricalised and performative nature of life – a fact Ervin Goffman (1959) hints at in *The Presentation of the Self in Everyday Life*. If gender is an act, then there is no reason why men's performance of female gender or vice versa should raise any eyebrows since nothing about femininity or masculinity is natural; it is observing, learning and repeating acts and behaviours culturally sanctioned as feminine and masculine. But that aside, the question, however, remains why men in these two cultures monopolise the art and instruments of representation, why do they not want women to represent themselves or the men as the latter are able to do, and why do they deny women access to the public space and thus to public speaking?

Looking at a majority of African societies and their forms of cultural representation, and in particular the two performance forms being used here as examples of the denial of the right of self-representation to women, it is obvious that the denial of the right to represent themselves is an integral element of male domination in patriarchal societies. This is still very much the situation in Igbo and Bamana cultures as nothing has changed in both societies nor in their main forms of theatrical performance. There is no doubt that within these social settings and their associated cultural practices, the fear of what the marginalized groups could do if given the freedom to occupy and make use of the public space is at the root of structures of repression that have been put in place, including theatrical performances and all other forms of cultural and artistic expression and representation.

The powerful and influential position of the spirits who are believed to inhabit the masquerades in *Mmonwu* enables the theatre to be a strong political as well as social instrument of cultural and social ordering. Spirits are higher than humans in Igbo thought and therefore they are never challenged by the latter, with the result that characters, and therefore the actors who perform them, become very effective mouthpieces for male hegemonic ideologies and discourses. In the past and up to a point still today, the masquerades were and are used to pass judgement on people, as well as to physically discipline them. They have remained the upholders of social morality and law, presenting what is right or wrong, and what images and behaviours that are socially approved. Because the judgements and moral injunctions which they give are perceived to be coming from the spirits, they are never questioned. The fact that contained in these injunctions are the male constructed images specified for women, and the fact that this is done by the men alone is usually culturally glossed over. Also, the fact that these roles, responsibilities and expected modes of behaviour and the codes and injunctions through which they are circulated in society are the way that men want women to act and see themselves is not even considered, and surprisingly, not even by women themselves. The same is true of the representations of social types in Bamana society by the male actors in the *Kote-tlon* performances. The fact that a sizeable proportion of the characters in the sketches are women and that the way they are represented and the way they are expected to behave are those conceived of by men does not appear to be an issue.

To be able to represent oneself is a major step towards an individual's liberation. History has shown that contexts of oppressions, exploitation and subjection are usually also contexts in which there is a denial of self-representation. The colonial and slave contexts in the New World were very good examples. The ability to represent one's self transforms an individual from a passive object into an active subject. In patriarchal societies such as the Bamana and Igbo, in which women are more often than not objects of and vehicles for men's desires and manipulation, they tend to be spoken about and for, but not by or for themselves. The construction and representation of women in Bamana and Igbo societies is by and through the male perspective - the images of women which circulate in the public domain are those based on the way men see and want women to be and not the way the women really are or feel about themselves.

Thus, it is not surprising that most of the skits in the *Kote-tlon* are very critical of female characters who show they have a mind of their own, an opinion or go against the behaviours expected of them. And in the Nkpor *Mmonwu* performances, especially in the Ayaka and Osonigwe satiric masquerades who compose and gleefully sing derogatory songs about stubborn, strong-willed and physically strong female characters. To be a physically strong woman is construed and presented negatively as in the song about the wife who gets the better of her husband in a domestic scuffle. In both theatre traditions, on the other hand, the virtues of the woman who knows and accepts her place is extolled and she is presented as the ideal woman. That ideal of womanhood, of course, usually means docility and submission to the authority of fathers, uncles, husbands or brothers. Of the three *kote-tlon* skits watched in Markala, two were about domestic scenes in which there were more female characters than there were males, yet the story was still woven around the husband in Sketch One and around the father and the lover in Sketch Two. The first skit was about a polygamous household and its fractious relationships, especially the bickering and bitching between the co-wives, and the second, more or less a sequel to Skit One, was about the father, the daughter and her lover, in which the daughter merely served as a backdrop for the father and lover who play out their antagonisms by having a go at each other. From the two sketches, it was clear that the women were deliberately presented in such a way to suggest that they had no life or existence outside that circumscribed and defined by their husbands (Mariamoufin and Nyebaje in Skit One) or lovers or fathers (Jeneba in the second skit). Their roles in the narratives were only as foils or as recipients of the actions of their male counterparts; in short, they were acted upon rather than acting in the narratives about their own lives.

Mmonwu sketches are no different in their representation of women as objects of men's desire and control. In fact, the Ayaka masquerades who compose and sing satiric songs about people in the town as a means of correcting deviant or unacceptable behaviour compose songs very critical of strong minded women who have the upper hand in their relationship with their husbands, and meanwhile such husbands are satirized as being weak while the women are presented as unusual or 'different'. In general, the ideal woman is presented as one who exists for her man. This study of the Nkpor *Mmonwu* tradition could not identify in the corpus of female characters strong independent women with equal status as their male counterparts. In the *Ochammili* performance, of the family of about ten members, there were only two female characters, a mother and a daughter. The mother's role was simply to support her husband; however, this was not in an active sense of helping him to run the affairs of the family. Her support came mainly in how she behaved, dressed and danced both to please her husband and to enhance his standing in the eyes of the public. This family outing consisted of the Nna Mmuo (Father) displaying his wealth which included his two exotic pets, Ochammili (Giraffe) and Anukaibie (Zebra), his array of police guards, his own private Ezeikolobia (huntsman), the family Onuku (Fool), an obligatory foreigner represented by Mmonwu Awusa, Nne Mmuo (Mother) and Adamma (Daughter). As with the pets, all these characters too were on display. Together, including his wife and daughter who were very finely dressed as part of this display, they represent a measure of Nna Mmuo's wealth. The two female characters (of course played by male actors) were as colourfully attired as the Giraffe and Zebra, and Nna Mmuo constantly used copious self-referential gestures to proudly announce to the world his ownership and control of everything and everyone within his household. All of them belonged to him and they helped to enhance his status. This performed attitude very clearly reflects an underlying tendency in Igbo culture to treat women as property which can be owned and exchanged by and between men. In the performance, Nne Mmuo and Adamma 'belong' to Nna Mmuo and he is meant to have control over them (Fig. 2).

Fig. 2 Nna Mmuo (left) leading Nne Mmuo out to the arena

The image of woman as something or someone to be shown off as an indicator of a man's wealth and social standing is very much a part of Bamana and Igbo iconography – for when a woman looks good, healthy and well-fed, it is because her husband or father provides for her. But, ironically, it is never the other way round, even if everybody in the community knows a husband is lazy and that it is the wife who works to feed and clothe her family, the man still gets praise for it. The image of a woman who can take care of herself, though not disapproved of, is not one found freely circulating in the public domain and in performances. In fact, such a woman is going against the grain, and thus a threat to the normal order of things. And by reinforcing this objectified and passive image of woman, by subtly disapproving of or suppressing the alternative image of the free-willed, active, thinking, doing and achieving woman, *Kote-tlon* and *Mmonwu* performances contribute greatly in denying agency and subject positions to women. In this way a subjectivity which the patriarchal social order denies them is made to appear normal and natural in *Koteba* and *Mmonwu* performances. In the latter, this exclusion from active participation and denial of agency is presented as having been sanctified by the gods, while in the former the exclusion and denial are attributed to the social institution of marriage and the biological process of having children.

Conclusion

In most illusionistic forms of theatre, according to Augusto Boal (1979), the spectator relinquishes his/her power of analysing and representing reality by delegating the responsibility to act to the actor; the latter then has the authority, as it were, to speak on their behalf. And this is wholly true of *Koteba* and *Mmonwu* performances in which the actors become the mouthpieces of their respective societies as they subject their cultures to scrutiny and revision. The fact that there is an element of spirituality underpinning the two theatrical practices gives added power to the actors, who incidentally are only men. Boal also advocates the creation of a theatre in which everybody can act and everybody can watch at the same time. The theatre is a context and an instrument for interrogating cultures and their social processes, and it is in the act of questioning and critically looking at these social processes that schisms, irregularities and injustices can be identified and possibilities for change explored. In *Koteba* and *Mmonwu* theatres, women are not allowed to be agents in this process of questioning or critically engaging with culture and society. Rather, they are at the receiving end of men's engagement with culture, with men's interpretation of the world, and also with men's representations of the different, shifting and contesting identities within culture. Through the subjective eyes of men, women are asked to see themselves; and also through the biased voices of the men, women's position, roles, responsibilities, feelings and thoughts are represented in Bamana and Igbo theatrical performances.

Finally, it is important to point out here that the feminine gender which the male actors in these performances enact is essentially ideology driven and therefore strategically constructed:

> When spectators 'see' gender, they are seeing (and reproducing) the cultural signs of gender, and by implication, the gender ideology of a culture. Gender in fact provides a perfect illustration of ideology at work since 'feminine' and 'masculine' behavior usually appears to be a 'natural' - and thus fixed unalterable - extension of biological sex. (Diamond, 1996 quoted in Counsell and Wolf, 2001:79)

Femininity, as performed in *Koteba* and *Mmonwu* sketches, is a passive and submissive femininity, which reflects and at the same time reinforces the subjected and marginalized position of women in the patriarchal social structures of Bamana and Igbo societies. The femininity represented in *Koteba* and *Mmonwu* contrasts sharply with the active femininity which women themselves enact in their everyday lives and in other performances forms in these two cultures. In *Koteba* and *Mmonwu* performances the possibility of agency or a self-assertive and therefore potentially disruptive femininity is carefully underplayed or censored when present, or 'written' out of the performance texts altogether.

References

Arnoldi, M. J (1995), *Playing with Time: Art and Performance in Central Mali*. Bloomington, Indianapolis: Indiana University Press

Boal, Augusto (1979), *Theatre of the Oppressed*, London: Pluto Press

Brink, James (1977), 'Bamana Kote-tlon Theater' in *African Arts* 10/4

Brink, James (1978), 'Communicating Ideology in Bamana Rural Theatre Performance' in *Research in African Literatures* 9

Butler, Judith (1990), 'Performative Acts and Gender Construction: An Essay in Phenomenology and Feminist Theory' in Sue Ellen-Case (ed.) *Performing Feminisms: Feminist Critical Theory and Theatre*, Baltimore: John Hopkins University Press

Butler, Judith (1990), *Gender Trouble: Feminism and the Subversion of Identity*, London: Routledge

de Beauvoir, Simone (1973), *The Second Sex*, trans. E. M. Parshley, New York: Vintage Press

den Otter, Elisabeth et Keita, Mamadou (2002), *Sogo Bo: La Fette des Masques Bamanan*. Segou & Amsterdam: KIT Press (Institut Royal des Tropiques)

Diamond, Elin (1996), 'Brechtian Theory/Feminist Theory: Towards a Gestic Feminist Criticism' in C. Martin ed. *A Source Book of Feminist Theatre and Performance: On and Beyond the Stage*. London: Routledge

Enekwe, Ossie Onuora (1987), *Igbo Masks: The Oneness of Ritual and Theatre*. Lagos: Nigeria Magazine

Goffman, Ervin (1959), *The Presentation of the Self in Everyday Life*, New York: Doubleday

Imperato, P. J. (1994), 'The depiction of Beautiful Women in Malian Youth association Masquerades' in *African Arts* Vol. XXVII

Kerr, David (1995), *African Popular Theatre*, London: James Currey

Okagbue, Eseagba A (1993), Personal Interview, Nkpor

Okagbue, Osita (2007), *African Theatres and Performances*, London, New York: Routledge

Onyeneke, Augustine O (1987), *The Dead Among the Living: Masquerades in Igbo Society*. Nimo, Nigeria: Holy Ghost Congregation

Shevtsova, Maria (1993), *Theatre and Cultural Interaction*, Sydney: Sydney Studies in Society and Culture & the University of Sydney

Turner, Victor (1990), 'Are there Universals of Performance?' in Schechner, Richard & Appel, Willa eds. *By Means of Performance: Intercultural Studies of Theatre and Ritual* Cambridge: Cambridge University Press

AfTA Notice Board

African Performance Review
Vol.1 Nos 2&3 2007
pp130-138

K.W. DEXTER LYNDERSAY: AN OBITUARY TRIBUTE

Professor Dapó Adelugba
Ahmadu Bello University, Zaria, Nigeria

K.W. Dexter Lyndersay, a citizen of Trinidad and Tobago, was born on April 15, 1932 and he died on December 18, 2006, living vitally to the ripe age of seventy-four. He had his primary school education at Tranquillity Boy's Intermediate and his secondary school education at Queen's Royal College, both in Trinidad. Mr. Lyndersay graduated from the Kenneth Sawyer Goodman School of Drama at the Art Institute of Chicago with a Bachelor of Fine Arts (BFA) in 1964, and he obtained the Master of Fine Arts (MFA) at the Yale School of Drama, Yale University, U.S.A., in 1965. His MFA thesis was entitled "A Creative Arts Centre for Trinidad and Tobago." In addition to his BFA and MFA degrees, he also enrolled for the Certificate programme in Television at the Institute of Music, Dance and Theatre in Brussels, Belgium, in 1970. Dexter Lyndersay was an academic editor for the Caribbean Entry to 'The Americas' volume of Don Rubin's World Encyclopaedia of Contemporary Theatre, a 1995 publication of the International Theatre Institute (I.T.I.). He also served as Copy Editor for Dr Rhoda Reddock's edited book, The Creolization of Minorities in the Caribbean, a work published by the Institute of Social and Economic Research (ISER), University of the West Indies, Trinidad, in 1995.

Essentially a technical theatre director and theatre technologist, he used his initial training as a theatre technician intelligently and he broadened his vision to embrace the fields of playwriting/play adaptation, directing and acting (which he always enjoyed, although he did not have much time for it, since he was constantly called upon to render his assistance in the crucial areas of production). Among his playwriting/play adapting and directorial credits are: "Mr. Three," adapted at Ibadan in 1971 from a novel of the same title by William Butler, "After One Time _ _ _ A Trinidad Wedding," which he wrote to celebrate his marriage to Danielle Moquette (later Dani Lyndersay) in Ibadan in 1972, "Mai Idris Alauma – 16th. Century African Warrior-King," which he wrote using available historical sources and directed in Kano and Maiduguri in Nigeria in 1973, Shaihu Umar (one of the highlights of his writing/production career) was adapted, with Umaru Ladan, from a novel of the same title by the former Nigerian Prime Minister, Head of State, Alhaji Sir Abubakar Tafawa Balewa. The Hausa language version of the adaptation was written by Umar Ladan who edited it for the Northern Nigerian Publishing Company, Zaria, Nigeria in 1974; the English version with Production Notes was largely written and edited by Dexter Lyndersay for Longman, London in 1975. It is a matter of significance that the Longman Shaihu Umar was a set-text for the West African School Certificate (WASC) Literature – in – English syllabus for 1988/89/90. Other plays adapted or written by Dexter Lyndersay are "Kolera Kolej," adapted by Femi Osofisan and Dexter Lyndersay from the former's novel of the same title, and staged at Ibadan in 1975, at Calabar in 1978 and in Trinidad in 1988; The Successor, written in collaboration with Okon Ekanem and Imaikop S. Orok and staged at Calabar in 1976; "Astray in the Mountain," an original Christmas play for children written by Dexter Lyndersay and staged at Uyo in 1983.

The following full-length children's plays were written in collaboration with his wife, Dani Lyndersay: "Space Trek," written and staged at Ibadan in 1969, "The Wizard of Oz," adapted from Frank Baum, and staged at Ibadan in 1970, "The Hobbit," adapted from J.R. Tolkein and staged at Ibadan in 1971; "Ruwan Bagaja (The Water of Cure)," adapted from Alhaji Abubakar Imam's work and staged in Kano in 1972, "Adamu and his Beautiful Wife," with school children writers, music composers, a musical adapted from Adamu da Kyakyawar Amayar Tasa, a Hausa folktale, staged in Hausa in Kano in 1974, and staged in English, based on a translation by Abdulkarim Mohammed Abdullahi, in Calabar in 1979. Dexter Lyndersay was co-playwright/director with Dani Lyndersay and members of Rebirth House in the production of "Blocks," a one-act play on Drug/Alcohol Demand Reduction, to launch Government Substance Abuse Prevention Week in Trinidad and Tobago in 1991.

Apart from his work in the combined fields of playwriting/play adaptation and production, he was also director of a good number of full-length plays and one-act plays. These include his stage adaptation of C.L.R. James's The Black Jacobins, which had its world premiere at the University of Ibadan Arts Theatre in 1967, Aar? Akogun, a Nigerian adaptation William of Shakespeare's Macbeth, which he jointly adapted with the Nigerian playwright, Wale Ogunyemi, with whom he co-directed the adaptation for the University of Ibadan in 1968; The Blacks by Jean Genet which he single-handedly directed for the University of Ibadan Arts Theatre stage in 1975. The following year he directed the premiere production of Samson O. Amali's Onugbo M'loko, which he revised and re-staged as a dance drama at the University of Ibadan Arts Theatre. At the University of Calabar in 1977 he directed Bertolt Brecht's A Man's a Man, which he revised for its African premiere production, substituting the Army for the Liberation of the Peoples of Africa (ALPA) for the Army of the British Empire. In 1981 he directed once again an adaptation of William Shakespeare's Macbeth, with which he was particularly creative in the roles of the three Witches and Hecate which he built from the local lore of the Efik, the Ibibio and the Annang of South-Eastern Nigeria. In September 1985 he directed Agbo Sikuade's "Egun Lapampa," which was produced by CORNUCOPIA in collaboration with the Nigerian Federal Department of Culture/Archives at the National Arts Theatre in Lagos, Nigeria.

Among the one-act plays which Dexter Lyndersay gave deft direction are the following: Lindsay Eseoghene Barrett's And After This We Heard of Fire, Cecily Waite – Smith's Africa Slingshot, Stanley French's Ballad of a Man and a Dog, Errol Hill's Dance Bongo, Freddie Kissoon's Zingay, Neville Labastide's One for the Road, Tewfik al – Hakim's Not a Thing out of Place, Ogonna Agu's "House of Death," Kole Omotoso's "The Golden Curse," which was revised and published as The Curse, Edward Albee's The American Dream and Ed Bullins' A Son Come Home. He compiled two sets of excerpts for staged dramatic readings; in 1976, "The Literature of Black America," consisting of excerpts from the genres of drama, poetry and prose, was specially prepared by Lyndersay for the African American History Week and staged at USIA Lagos and Ibadan. In 1982 he did a compilation of multi-ethnic poetry from Africa, America and the Caribbean which he staged in Victoria, British Columbia, Canada and which he entitled "Black: From Womb to Tomb." A modified version of this compilation was staged at the University of Cross River State (now University of Uyo) in 1985. He spent the larger part of his adult life as technical director and all-round theatre teacher, scholar and theatre trainer in Nigeria, and in particular in four Nigerian Universities, viz., the University of Ibadan (1966-1972, 1974-1976), Ahmadu Bello University (at its Kano Centre for Nigerian Cultural Studies base) (1972-1974), University of Calabar, whose Department of Theatre Arts he founded and led (1976-1982) and the University of Cross River State, now University of Uyo (1982-1983).

In addition to his creative writings, Dexter Lyndersay also took time off to do some purely academic writing. He wrote "Look to the Ladies-African Witches as Shakespeare's Weird Sisters (Macbeth): Two Versions of Shakespeare's play, one with witches according to Yorubaland, Southwest Nigeria, the other with witches according to Calabar, Southeast Nigeria." This was published in On-Stage Studies, Journal of the Colorado Shakespeare Festival, University of Colorado, No. 7, Fall 1983. In 1984 Dexter Lyndersay wrote another academic article based on his directorial work, "Performing Jean Genet's The Blacks in Nigeria (Directing the African Premiere)." This was commissioned and accepted by Recherche Pedagogie et Culture), Audecam, Paris, France. His 1985 article," Text and Sub-text-I: Ogonna Agu's House of Death was accepted for publication by KIABARA, Journal of the Humanities, University of Port Harcourt. Another essay entitled "A Contradiction within a Paradox: Problems in Preparing a Revision of Bertolt Brecht's A Man's a Man in the Context of an

African Liberation Army" was published in 1988 in Comparative Literature and Foreign Languages in Africa, a Festschrift for William Feuser edited by 'Tunde Okanlawon of the University of Port Harcourt. In 1992 he wrote another article, "Aspects of Performance Environments in Nigeria," which was commissioned and accepted for Modern African Drama and Theatre jointly edited by James Amankulor and Carl R. Mueller. In 1997 his essay, "Theatre Architecture in Nigeria" was commissioned and accepted for the Nigeria Entry in Don Rubin's World Encyclopaedia of Contemporary Theatre – Africa, a work in a series sponsored by the International Theatre Institute (I.T.I.).

In the 1990s and in the early years of the 2000 decade Dexter Lyndersay lived and worked in the West Indies and was based in Trinidad/Tobago where he was Director of the National Theatre for some years. In the last eighteen years of his life he was very active in the educational drama and theatre movement of the West Indies and he helped in the formulation of theatre-in-education syllabuses. He was also active in the Theatre-in-Education (TIE) schools performances. Among his productions in this sector a few may be mentioned: Wole Soyinka's The Swamp Dwellers which he staged in 1992," Trevor Rhone's Old story Time, which he produced in 1991, A Brighter Sun" which he adapted from Samuel Selvon's novel and staged in 1997, "The Day the World Almost Came to an End," adapted from Crayton's short story and staged in 1998, "Bella Makes Life," an adaptation of Lorna Goodison's short story, staged in 1998, "Green Days by the River," adapted from Michael Anthony's novel and staged in 2005, Henry V by William Shakespeare staged in 1992, Poems from Collections: "Facing the Sea," staged in 1992/93, and "Sunsong Tide Rising," staged in 1998/99.

Lyndersay was undoubtedly an all round man of the theatre and a connoisseur of the arts. He acted in a good number of productions – as Tajomaru, the Bandit in F. & M. Kanin's Rashomon staged at the University of Ibadan Arts Theatre in 1969, Eddie, the Butler in Slawimir Mrozek's Tango, also at the University of Ibadan Arts Theatre in 1970, Aweri Eleven in the film version of Wole Soyinka's Kongi's Harvest directed by the famous African American actor and director, Ossie Davis and Wole Soyinka and produced by Calpenny (Nigeria) Films.

Dexter Lyndersay was at different times a voice to be reckoned with in media arts. He was co-creator, director and host, with Dani Lyndersay, of Children's Theatre Time, a weekly half – hour series totalling twenty-six episodes for Western Nigeria Television (WNTV) in 1971/72 and a set of thirteen episodes for Radio – Television Kaduna (RTK) in 1973. As radio host, Lyndersay was creator/compere for NOW YOU HAS-JAZZ, first Trinidad & Tobago Jazz programme for Radio Trinidad as far back as in 1956, over five decades ago, He was also radio host and Creator/ Compere of DEXTER'S DECK, a Jazz programme prepared for and broadcast on Western Nigeria Broadcasting Service (WNBS), Ibadan, Nigeria in 1966. As Freelance BBC Radio Interviewer, Lyndersay compered TODAY, with Jack de Mannio and CARIBBEAN MAGAZINE in London in 1966 and 1967. Lyndersay was also Creator/Host in 1972/73 of a Radio Playwriting Demonstration Course, 20 programmes in English, and, with Umaru Ladan as Host, 6 programmes in Hausa. This course, which spread over two quarters of the 1972/73 academic session, was specially prepared for Ahmadu Bello University (Zaria) Educational Extension Services, even though the A.B.U Performing Arts programme was then domiciled in Kano.

Dexter Lyndersay was, among his other attributes, a serious-minded and careful photographer as far back as the 1950s and 1960s and he produced Jazz, Folk, Choral and Calypso Record Jacket Covers and Liner Notes. From 1962 to 1965 Lyndersay was Theatre Photographer for the Art Institute of Chicago (1962-64) and for Yale University (1964-65). Regarding the latter, Lyndersay produced the Yale University Drama School Brochure Cover Photograph based on the school façade.

Among his other achievements Lyndersay was often appointed as Judge for artistic and cultural competitions and festivals, only a few of which will be mentioned here. In 1991 he was Chief Judge for a playwriting competition, sponsored by T&T National Petroleum Marketing Company, for the National Drama Association of Trinidad and Tobago (NDATT). Also in 1991 he was one of the Judges for Playwriting and Short Story competitions for Trinidad & Tobago Unified Teacher's Association (TTUTA). In 1995 he was one of the Judges for T&T Best Village Finals in the Concert Category in Trinidad. Also in 1965 he was Chief Judge in Barbados for the T&T Secondary School Drama Festival. In 2004 (to cite a more recent example), Lyndersay was Overseas Judge for the Speech and Drama Finals of the National Independence Festival of Creative Arts (NIFCA) sponsored by the Barbados National Cultural Foundation.

Dexter Lyndersay, Arts Director of Theatre Arts, a professorial position with emphasis on creativity and artistic output, was Consultant for several Theatre Architecture/ Lighting Layout Projects on behalf of the client in each case: for the Creative Arts Centre in Jamaica (Architect Hendrickse), University of the West Indies, Mona in 1965, two theatres, one of which was proscenium and the other, arena (in a reserved portion of lobby space; for Trinidad, he was Consultant for Naparima Bowl I (Architect Barcant) in 1965 and in 1989 for Naparima Bowl II, Outdoor and Indoor Theatres – back – to – back: he was Stage Lighting Layout Designer and Architectural Consultant. In 1990 for the National Festival Centre, for Uriah Butler H/way, Lyndersay did a Design & Planning Brief for the National Architects' Competition – 3 Theatres (Music, Drama & Steelband) with Works Department Architects and Consultants, led by Architect Ken Dublin. In 1992 he was Director of Venues and Infrastructure for the famous festival, Carifesta V, and in 1999 was Theatre Architecture/Lighting Layout Consultant for the Performing Arts Theatre, Dr. Joao Havelange Centre of Excellence.

In Nigeria, where Dexter Lyndersay's contributions have been most notable and where he spent twenty years (1966-1985) of his mature career years, he was Consultant at different times to seven University Theatres and four State Theatres: viz., the University of Ibadan Arts Theatre, where he re-organized the Stage Lighting Layout in 1966, the Western State (later Oyo State) Cultural Centre, where the present writer, as Chairman of the Oyo State Council for Arts and Culture, invited Lyndersay and other experts in theatre architecture, theatre technology and theatre design to advise, in a Consultancy capacity, during the 1977-1983 period; Abdullahi Bayero University, Kano (B.U.K.), where Lyndersay gave consultancy advice to Kano State architects and made an input in the erection of two theatres – indoor and outdoor (back – to – back)-in 1974; University of Lagos, Lagos State, where he served as Consultant to Architect Griffin & Interplan Associates in Lagos, Nigeria and Rome, Italy in 1973. Two theatres emerged from this collaboration: a 2,000-seat theatre and a 510-seat theatre.

For the Borno State Ministry of Culture Zoo Outdoor Theatre, Lyndersay was a Consultant to the Works Architect (Office & Site) in 1973. Also in the same year he was a Consultant to the North-Western (now Sokoto) State Ministry of Culture and he was a Consultant to the Works Architect (Office & Site), and they built a 2,000 – seat theatre for the State.

For the University of Calabar, which was his main base during his years of pioneer Headship of its Department of Theatre Arts, he was Consultant to Architect Asuquo for its 2,000 – seat theatre from the Drawing Board. Lyndersay was Audience Seating and Stage Lighting Layout Designer for the conversion of three University spaces into theatre venues, such as,

The Assembly Hall (while the Main Theatre was being built),

The Theatre Arts Department Courtyard which was converted to a 'Black-Box' Theatre,

The Outdoor Garden Theatre on the grass near the Theatre Arts Department Building.

Lyndersay was Designer (including custom adaptations from extant drawings) and Construction Supervisor for portable, demountable, modular wooden stages and bleachers & sets of graded, collapsible platforms to facilitate travelling theatre activity. For Lagos State University, Badagry, Lyndersay prepared drawings for the reorganization of existing theatre spaces; he did a design (with basic sketches) for a 'black box' theatre with its administration spaces. He designed a four-year Theatre Arts Curriculum with a Stage Lighting Course Description.

With the initial success at Ibadan in the 1966-1972 period and the follow-up successes at the Ahmadu Bello University Zaria at its performing arts base in Kano (1972-1974), he made an impact on the technical theatre, scenery and lighting design and execution in several university theatres and state theatres in Nigeria. In sum, he was technical director and/or scenery/lighting designer and executant for over 250 stage productions in several Nigerian towns and cities during a total of twenty-one academic years (1966-1987). During this period Dexter Lyndersay established himself not only as a trained and gifted theatre technician/technologist/designer, but also as an educator and administrator at the University of Ibadan, Ahmadu Bello University (Kano Campus), University of Calabar and University of Cross River State (now University of Uyo), and he developed and taught a variety of courses including Theatre Arts Theory/ Practice, Technical Theatre (Stage Lighting and Scenery Construction), Theatre Forms, Directing/Writing for Stage/Radio/Television/Film, Stage Management, Theatre Architecture, Functional Design, Theatre/Studio Administration, and Introduction to Drama Criticism. Lyndersay was the Acting Director of the School of Drama (now Department of Theatre Arts), University of Ibadan from 1967 to 1969; he was a Senior Research Fellow Drama at the Centre for Nigerian Cultural Studies, Ahmadu Bello University (ABU) Kano from 1972 to 1974. He returned to the University of Ibadan as Senior Arts Fellow for two academic sessions, teaching a variety of courses and serving as Project Director for the reorganized University of Ibadan semi-professional Performing Arts Company, the Unibadan Masques (1974-1976). He was invited by the Vice-Chancellor, University of Calabar, Professor E.A. Ayandele, in 1976 to serve as Arts Director and founding Head for a new Department of Theatre Arts, a position which he occupied from 1976 to 1982. He continued to serve as Arts Director at Calabar until he moved over to the University of Cross River State (now University of Uyo) to do more pioneer work. At Calabar, Lyndersay was not only the Head of the Department of Theatre Arts; he was also the Artistic Director of the Calabar University Theatre (CUT), which he founded and developed, hiring dancers, musicians, drummers and a seven – piece modern musical band to augment regular student actors and dancers. CUT had the honour of staging two Command Performances for Nigerian Heads of State.

It may at this juncture be necessary to point out that Dexter Lyndersay's artistic career did not begin in Nigeria. He had, as a young man, made some impact on the artistic and cultural life of Trinidad during the 1950s and 1960s. For example, he was Dancer/Stage Manager/Property Master for Beryl McBurnie's Little Carib Theatre from 1953 to 1961. He was Art Director for Liner Notes and Photographs, RCA Record Jackets from 1958 to 1961, and in 1961 he was RCA Artists Celebrity Concert Director for Managing Director Leslie Lucky-Samaroo. From 1958 to 1961 he was Weekly Columnist in the field of Jazz/Popular Music for <u>The Nation</u> under the Editorship of the famous C.L.R. James. For a period of eleven years, from 1950 to 1961, he was a Civil Servant in the Ministry of Education and Culture, his last duty post being in the Culture Division. Among other duties he was "Theme Concert" Director at Queen's Hall for Conference Delegates. In 1965 he served briefly as Technical Theatre Tutor for the

University of the West Indies Extra-Mural Unit (now known as School of Continuing Studies).

Since his return to his native home in Trinidad in 1988 he held a variety of leadership and pioneering posts. From 1988 to 1991 he was Director of Culture in the Division of Culture, Ministry of Youth, Sports, Culture and Creative Arts. One of his main achievements during his tenure was a major re-organization of Best Village in 1989. From 1991 to 1992 he was Project Designer/Director of Youth Crossroads, a people – oriented programme (POP) using drama techniques for problem – solving for 12 – 18 year–olds, after an attempted *coup d' état* in 1990. In 1992 he served as Drama Techniques Workshop Leader for YTEPP Tutors' Training Course.

All through his richly endowed and successful career Dexter Lyndersay was indeed an official cultural representative for Trinidad and Tobago at home and abroad. In the United Kingdom during the Commonwealth Arts Festival in London/ Croydon / Glasgow in 1965, he was Stage Manager/Technical Director for the Trinidad and Tobago entry which was <u>Man Better Man</u> by the late Trinidadian playwright/academic, Errol Hill.

In Senegal, West Africa, Lyndersay was very active at the First World Festival 'des Arts Negres' in 1966. He was Technical Director and Lighting Designer to the Nigeria contingent for Wole Soyinka's <u>Kongi's Harvest</u> and for Geoffrey Axworthy/Demas Nwoko's production of a stage adaptation of Nkem Nwankwo's novel, <u>Danda,</u> which was made into a dance – drama, and I.K. Dairo's Highlife Band. For the same World Festival of Black Arts Lyndersay was appointed Artistic Director for the Trinidad and Tobago contingent by His Excellency Reginald Dumas, then Trinidad & Tobago Ambassador to Ethiopia, and he superintended Rudolph Charles' West Indian Tobacco Desperadoes Steelband, Julia Edwards' Dance Troupe, The Mighty Terror (translations into French by Ambassador Dumas), and Calypso band with Charles at the piano, George Goddard, then president, Pan Trinbago, John Cupid, MP David Pitt.

Also at the 1966 Dakar World Festival Lyndersay was appointed Stage Lighting Designer, through USA and UK Ambassadors' requests, for Duke Ellington and his Orchestra (USA) and for two UK plays: <u>Wind Versus Polygamy</u> by Obi Egbuna of Nigeria and <u>The Voyage</u> by Horace James of Trinidad and Tobago – all at the Daniel Sorano Theatre in Dakar. The Duke of Ellington Orchestra also gave a performance at the 12, 000 – seat Stadium in Dakar.

In 1977 for the Second World Festival of Black and African Arts and Culture (FESTAC ' 77) which took place in Lagos, Dexter Lyndersay was appointed, from his University of Calabar base, through the Trinidad and Tobago High Commission, Artistic Director of the Trinidad and Tobago contigent consisting of the Catelli All Stars Steelband, the Morne Diable Best Village Folk Performers, The Mighty Sparrow with Trinidad Troubadours, Sidney Hill and the Government Film Unit, Mr. John Cupid,

M.P. David Pitt – the performers on stage, together, at the 5,000-seat (fully sold out) National Arts Theatre, Iganmu, Lagos on "TRINIDAD & TOBAGO NIGHT." Trinidad All Stars and Mighty Sparrow gave separate performances at FESTAC 'FRINGE' in the University of Lagos 2,000-seat Auditorium.

In April 1990 in West Germany (Lingen) Dexter Lyndersay was leader of a Culture – Ministry – approved production of Children's Theatre of Trinidad and Tobago, a BWIA – sponsored Private Entry to the First World Children's Theatre Festival.

Consistent with his aesthetic tastes and artistic leanings Dexter Lyndersay's hobbies up till his transition were the appreciation of Jazz/Calypso, Folk and Classical Music, Reading, Prose Writing and Photography.

Dexter Lyndersay was married to Australian/Dutch born Danielle Moquette (now Dr. Dani Lyndersay) who is herself a theatre scholar, artist, designer, educator, theatre trainer and performer. The marriage is blessed with two children, Adam Lyndersay and Sean Lyndersay.

May our colleague's soul rest in perfect peace.

The Search for Definitions:
Critical Perspectives on African Theatre and Performance

(Report of the 1st International Conference of the African Theatre Association (AfTA) held at Goldsmiths, University of London, 30 August-1 September, 2007)

Francis Ndu Anike
London

The 1st annual conference of the African Theatre Association (AfTA), as intended, provoked so much questions, debates and discussions. At the end, all the delegates signed up for the 2008 conference, as well as registering as members of AfTA.

Dr. Osita Okagbue, President of AfTA, in his welcome address had jokingly hinted that the accepted wisdom, especially in western scholarly circles, was that Africans can never do anything for themselves. Giving examples from his early teaching days in the United Kingdom, he argued that the struggle for identity and the marginalization of African theatre and its practitioners and scholars within European academia will remain for as long as those who hold the purse strings or make decisions about curriculum policy with regard to African theatre scholarship and practice are not indigenous. These include: the research councils who through their funding authorize what is researched; the education planners who decide what course/subjects are taught; the Arts Council which ensures what is performed; the publishing houses who determine what research makes it into the public domain; and of course, it also includes the young people at British High Commissions and embassies, especially those in Africa, who routinely and arbitrarily refused visas to delegates who wished to attend the conference, including a professor of theatre who probably trained in the United Kingdom or the United States of America.

A truly eclectic mix of papers was offered over the three days which the conference lasted; in all, twenty-one papers were presented and one performance installation. Most of the papers presented echoed Dr Okagbue's 'What is African Performance and Theatre?', the question with which he began his opening address. In his speech, Dr Okagbue had suggested that a critical perspective of African theatre and the biggest issue facing it was one of defining its context within its own framework. This argument was taken up in Dr. Esiaba Irobi's paper, *The Problem of Postcolonial Theory: Re-Theorizing African Theatre and Performance in the Age of Globalization*, on the last day in which he argues for a new vernacular theory derived from the languages and cultures the performances originate from. This argument was previously buttressed in Professor Robert Gordon's *Fugard in Performance* presented on the opening day in which, in analysing a production of *Sizwe Bansi* by Peter Brook, he argued the performance lacked soul because it had no link with the culture of the play and its subject.

Dr Mercy Ntangaare, the keynote speaker from Uganda who spoke on Day Two, argued that while the quest for definition goes on, African theatre has remained a progressive practice because it is not just art but also a service. Dr. F. Ndu Anike's *Masquerade as Theatre*, Ikechukwu Nwaru's *Study of Omenimo*, Gbenga Windapo's *Dynamics of Sato Dance*, Dr Victor Ukaegbu's *Mediating Space and Venue* and Dr Sam Kasule's *Changing Concepts* all explored this unique process of theatre as service in the African milieu. Ms Ijeoma Akunna in her paper, *Dance as Mental Therapeutic in the African Experience: Beyond the Speculation*, went a step further to propose that African dance is therapeutic and curative by nature and Ms Uche Hassan in *Costume and Make-Up as Medium for Cultural Expression in Stage Performance* proposed that costume and make-up in performance are signifiers of African cultural identities. This position was borne out in Chikukuango Cuxima-Zwa's *Angola Body Painting in Britain: A Contemporary Cultural Identity* where the actor becomes the subject, object and context of the performance.

In *World of Drama*, Reginald Ofodile examined the social disparities among the Creoles of Sierra Leone as presented in the writings of Sarif Easmon, while Bisi Adigun's *The Vulture and the Ape* questioned Wole Soyinka's unacknowledged and uncelebrated pioneering role as an intercultural dramatist by arguing that long before Peter Brook's and Ariane Mnouchkine's *The Mahabharata* and *L'Indiade* respectively, Soyinka and other African dramatists had been adapting Western 'classics and mixing the foreign with the familiar'. Chikwendu Anyanwu's paper, on the other hand, concerned itself with inter-textual and inter-genre adaptation as he called for contemporary African writers to adapt classical African novels for the stage. He explored the challenges he faced in the *Kingdom of the Mask*, a stage adaptation of Chinua Achebe's *A Man of the People*. Victor Ladan's *Transcribing the Lexicon of "Culture of Silence" in Theatre for Development'* urged the practice to 're-image itself from being a problem-solving practice to that of confidence-builder for affected communities', while Sam Kasule's *Simbawo Akati* looked at the changing concepts of 'popular theatre and performance in Uganda' beyond its present "finished product" approach. Prof. Duro Oni's *Assessment of Design and Technology* courses in Nigerian universities highlighted the challenges facing theatre arts students wishing to acquire skills in computer-aided-designs. He posited that theatre practice in Nigeria and indeed, most African countries, was 'poor' *ala* Grotowski but that the process was a victim of circumstance and not design. The conference discussion in reaction to the paper suggested cross-departmental collaborations whereby Engineering, for example, will assist Theatre Arts.

Professor Dap? Adelugba's keynote speech, read by Osita Okagbue, explored the challenges of building and sustaining creative associations and exhorted AfTA to become a positive emblem and outlet for present and upcoming African scholars.

The final keynote speaker, Peter Badejo, OBE, encapsulated the difficulties of African theatre and performance practice abroad. He identified irregular funding as the bane of practitioners, but delegates argued that if most of the major practitioners would club together to make funding applications, things might turn out different. It was also proposed that practitioners should explore alternative means of funding for African arts, including seeking out the small, round-the-corner African businesses. Peter Badejo showcased his majestic dance drama, *Sango*, to general approval.

The three-day conference was pieced together by Sarahleigh Castelyn's *Proudly South African* or *How I Chased the Rainbow and Bruised My Knee*, an installation piece of poems, narratives and pictures. *Proudly South African* provoked questions on what it means to be white and African. There was a welcome presentation by playwright/dramaturg, Gabriel Gbadamosi (an AHRC Research Fellow at Goldsmiths), Akim Mogaji of BBC World Service Trust of their recent creative writing project in Nigeria entitled *Wetin Dey*, which also provoked much discussion among the conference participants.

As delegates pointed out in response to Babafemi Babatope's *Muse, Mood and Creativity*, the African child has been born, his destiny is decided; all that remains is for this child to be given a name that will not only define it as an entity but will be the embodiment of what will give it a place and a reference in the theatre world. The African Theatre Association, its conferences and its journal, the *African Performance Review* (*APR*), are poised to answer the challenge thrown by Dr Okagbue's welcome speech; to sustain and promote knowledge and excellence among African scholars at home and in the Diaspora. Hopefully, very soon, this will no longer be a contentious question.

142